Joseph of Arimathea

Garland Medieval Texts
Number 5

Garland Medieval Texts

A.S.G. Edwards
General Editor

Number 1:
The Commonplace Book of Robert Reynes of Acle:
An Edition of Tanner MS407
Edited by Cameron Louis

Number 2:
The Isle of Ladies
or The Ile of Pleasaunce
Edited by Anthony Jenkins

Number 3:
The Creacion of the World:
A Critical Edition and Translation
Edited and Translated by Paula Neuss

Number 4:
Scotish Feilde and Flodden Feilde:
Two Flodden Poems
Edited by Ian F. Baird

Number 5:
Joseph of Arimathea
A Critical Edition
Edited by David A. Lawton

Joseph of Arimathea
A Critical Edition

edited by
David A. Lawton

GARLAND PUBLISHING, INC.
NEW YORK & LONDON
1983

Copyright © 1983 by David A. Lawton
All rights reserved

Library of Congress Cataloging in Publication Data
Joseph, of Arimathea.
  Joseph of Arimathea : a critical edition.

  (Garland medieval texts ; no. 5)
  Bibliography: p.
  1. Grail—Legends. 2. Joseph, of Arimathea—Legends.
I. Lawton, David A., 1948–   . II. Title. III. Series.
PR2007.J67 1983   821.1   81-22190
ISBN 0-8240-9448-4

Printed on acid-free, 250-year-life paper
Manufactured in the United States of America

For Elizabeth Salter

Contents

Acknowledgments • ix

INTRODUCTION
    The Manuscript and Its Format • xiii
    The Alliterative Question: Style, Date and Dialect • xxi
    The Source • xxix
    The Text • xxxviii
    Joseph of Arimathea in England • xxxix
    Notes to the Introduction • xliii
    Select Bibliography • liii

***JOSEPH OF ARIMATHEA:* THE TEXT • 1**
    Notes on the Text • 21
    Glossary • 47

Acknowledgments

I am grateful to the Keeper of Western Manuscripts, Bodleian Library, Oxford, for permission to make this edition from the Vernon manuscript, and I acknowledge a particular debt to Miss A.C. de la Mare for her courtesy and patience.

My thanks are also due to Amanda Beresford, for her valuable assistance with the glossary; to Sonia Jensen; to Professor H.L. Rogers and Dr. Geraldine Barnes, for their helpful and encouraging comments; to Lesley Lawton; to the Council of the Early English Text Society for permission to quote from EETS OS 44; to the Scolar Press; to Professor Tony Edwards, general editor of Garland Medieval Texts; and especially to Professor Derek Pearsall who, as so often, was liberal with his time and his ideas.

I acknowledge with pleasure a grant from the Research committee of the University of Sydney.

The greatest debt of all, to the late Professor Elizabeth Salter, can never be expressed adequately. Nobody who knew her could ever doubt that scholarship can be, in every sense, an art. Her continual inspiration over the last decade deserves a better tribute by far than this edition; and her untimely death in May of this year leaves me, as so many of her old students and friends, personally and intellectually bereaved. But I can at least begin to pay back what I owe.

David Lawton
University of Sydney, 1980

Introduction

Joseph of Arimathea has been edited only once before, by W.W. Skeat in 1871.[1] Skeat's edition is still in some respects useful but a new one requires little defense, if only in the scope for revised textual apparatus and glossary. Most importantly, however, the text is of special interest for charting "alliterative modes and affiliations in the fourteenth century."[2]

THE MANUSCRIPT AND ITS FORMAT

The sole extant copy of *Joseph* is found in folios 403^r-404^v of the Vernon manuscript, Bodleian Library MS Engl. Poet. a i. This is in every sense one of the major English vernacular manuscripts: it now weighs nearly 49 pounds, originally contained 414 folios (measuring approximately 15½ x 22½ inches) of which 73 have been lost,[3] and Miss Serjeantson's index runs to 377 items.[4] Apart from the Latin originals of some translated items, the anthology is monolingual, and its purpose is broadly devotional. Hence the manuscript's own Index calls the volume *Salus anime* or *Sowlehele*. It is, firstly, a comprehensive English legendary: the *South English Legendary* (folios 1^r-80^v) is supplemented by the smaller Vernon collection (folios 87^r-102^v),[5] the *Miracles of Our Lady* (folios 123^v-126^v, the last forty leaves of which have been removed for their illuminations), the rhymed alliterative poem *Susannah* (folios 316^v-317^r), and other hagiographic items. Secondly, it contains a uniquely full collection of devotional and other lyrics, including the famous Vernon collection with which the manuscript ends[6] (folios 407^r-412^r), and many longer homiletic or catechetic items in verse and of various types: the *Northern Homily Cycle* (folios 166^v-227^r), the *Prick of Conscience* (folios 264^v-283^v), an A-text of *Piers Plowman* (folios 394^r-401^v), the mildly sensational *Trental of St. Gregory* (of which these are two copies, folios 230^v-231^r and 303^r-303^v), along with other short didactic or affective items such as Grosseteste's *Castle of Love*[7] (folios 292^v-296^r). To this category of items belong homiletic romances such as *Ypotis* (folios 296^r-297^r), *Robert of Sicily* (folios 299^v-300^v), the *King of Tars* (folios 304^r-306^v), and - I shall argue - *Joseph*. Thirdly, the manuscript contains a fine collection of religious prose such as the *Stimulus Amoris* (folios 318^v-333^v), Rolle's *Form of Perfect Living* and *Ego Dormio* (folios 334^r-338^v), Book I of Hilton's *Scale of Perfection* (folios 342^v-353^r) and his *Epistle on the Mixed Life* (folios 353^r-355^v), *A Talking of the Love of God* (folios 367^r-371^v), and a version of the *Ancrene Wisse* (folios 371^v-391^v).[8]

The manuscript is the work of one scribe writing a fine and calligraphic Anglicana Formata, whose hand also appears in the closely related, and slightly later, Simeon manuscript (British Library Additional MS 22283). Discussion of the manuscript's provenance has centered on Lichfield[9] and, more recently, Cistercian abbies in Worcestershire, but there are objections to both proposed localizations.[10] It seems probable, from the scope of the Vernon manuscript as well as its relation with Simeon and other manuscripts, that the collection is the work of a major religious scriptorium.[11] The complex textual relations of items in Vernon and Simeon have led Dr. A.I. Doyle to the conclusion that "it is hard to imagine the total of separate sources utilized for V[ernon] as less than a couple of dozen of various formats, and possibly a good many more" (p.332). The manuscript used to be dated 1370-1380, but one of the lyrics in its final section refers to the Peasants' Revolt of 1381 and the earthquake of 1382, and on this and other textual grounds a date close to 1400 is now favored.[12]

Joseph belongs to what Dr. Doyle has called the fourth part of the manuscript, which contains all the prose items and ends with a prose redaction of the verse *Life of Adam and Eve* (folios 392^v-394^r), *Piers Plowman*, *Joseph* and *Judas and Pilate* from the *SEL* (folios 404^v-406^r). The format, as for the *SEL*, is in two columns rather than the three used for poems with short lines in the other four parts of the manuscript. There are about eighty lines in each column. It seems clear that the editor of the manuscript intended a "broad categorization of the material" (Doyle, p.332), but the later contents of part four are at first glance more than usually miscellaneous. *Judas and Pilate* appears to be an afterthought added, perhaps, when additional *SEL* material came to hand. Less plausibly, the *Life of Adam and Eve* may have been added for its connection with the legend of the True Cross. There is a case for seeing a similar motive behind the inclusion of *Joseph* late in this part of Vernon. Joseph of Arimathea was not incorporated into an English legendary until the sixteenth century, but interest in the saint had grown since Glastonbury propagandists around 1240 had claimed him as the protevangelist of Britain.[13] The Vernon director may have regarded his omission from the legendary material as unfortunate, and in this context he would have derived encouragement from references to Joseph in at least four of the manuscript's other items: the *Stimulus Amoris*,[14] two of the manuscript's three versions of the *Mirror of St. Edmund*,[15] in which Joseph's deposition of

Christ's body is prescribed as a proper subject for contemplation at evensong, and, more extensively and significantly, in the *Lamentation of Our Lady to St. Bernard*[16] (folios 286^v-288^r). In this last item, Christ's removal from the cross and burial by Joseph and Nicodemus are reported in Mary's own words. Joseph's initiative in demanding the corpse from Pilate (597-601) is emphasized, in accordance with the account in the *Evangelium Nicodemi*.[17] More important is the stress upon Joseph's perfect love of the dead Christ and his tenderness towards the bereaved mother:

> And Ioseph nome hym adoun
> Til I hym hedde, me þhouʒte ful late,
> Þe Iewes weoren alle ful feloun.
> Ioseph seide to me wiþ þate:
> 'To bringe him þe we ben ful boun.'
> Nichodemus þe nayles out drowʒ
> And Ioseph nom him in his Arm.
> Mi sone he louede wel inouʒ;
> He tok hym doun wiþouten harm
> And nom him of þe heiʒe bouʒ
> And leyde him softe in my Barm.
> His swete mouþ on me hit louh
> And ʒit ne was hit noþing warm.
>   (628-40; Vernon folio 288^r).

This is a convincing endorsement of Joseph's claim to legendary status, especially in a manuscript where (to judge, unhappily, from the three remaining leaves), the one major work to be given an extended and costly cycle of illumination was the *Miracles of Our Lady*.[18] A further justification of *Joseph*'s inclusion is discussed below (p.xxvii f.).

Unfortunately, the extant text of *Joseph* is incomplete: one leaf, folio 402, is missing. The leaf certainly contained the end of *Piers Plowman* and the beginning of *Joseph* and, given the abbreviated state of the manuscript's original index at this late stage, it is not impossible that an additional short item may also have been lost. Skeat estimated that 100 lines or so of the beginning of *Joseph* are missing, and this opinion has been repeated by later scholars. It rests, however, on a dubious assumption: that, because the Vernon copy of the *Piers Plowman* A Text is of such high quality, the manuscript would have included 'Passus XII.' However, A 'Passus XII' "was probably not in the archetype of the extant manuscripts";[19] and Professor Kane's statement of the case differs significantly from Skeat's:

> *Piers Plowman* is physically intact except for loss of
> its last leaf (fol. 402). This could have held 320
> lines, that is the 135-40 lines needed to finish
> Passus XI and at least 180 more. It could thus have
> accommodated the 117 lines of Passus XII as well as a
> beginning for the next item, *Joseph of Arimathea*. But
> since the Vernon text of the alliterative life of
> Joseph appears to be unique there is no way of
> determining how much of fol. 402 was originally
> occupied by *Piers Plowman*.
>
> (Kane, p.17).

I see no way to dissent from the logic of this. While there are literary grounds for hypothesis about the content of the lost beginning to *Joseph* (below, p. xxviii), there are no exact means of estimating its length.

The format and punctuation of *Joseph* is problematic. The Vernon scribe copies *Piers Plowman* in verse format, carefully pointing a medial caesura and occasional, non-metrical, stops in the lines. The same treatment is given to the item immediately following *Joseph*, *Judas and Pilate*. *Joseph*, however, is written in prose format throughout,[20] with punctuation similar to that of the York Register text of *Gaytryge's Sermon*[21] or the Cotton Caligula A xi manuscript of Laȝamon's *Brut*:[22]

> sire he seis. and soneᵑday is nouwe ₡ þenne alle lauh
> when an heiȝ. þat herden his wordes. Hit is two and fourti
> winter þei seiȝen. trewely forsoþe. siþen þou souȝtest þis
> put. and to prison eodest. Now I. þonke my lord seide
> Ioseph. þat lente me of his grace. me þinkeþ but þreo niȝt.
> al þis ilke þrowe.
>
> (folio 403ʳ, column a).

Skeat observes that many passages of *Joseph* are highly alliterative, and was in no doubt that this is an alliterative poem:

> I have said just above that the poem is written
> continuously, like prose. But that it is a genuine
> specimen of Alliterative verse was soon evident, and
> a little attention would soon have enabled me to
> divide it into lines of the right length. The scribe,
> however, has saved me the trouble, for he has marked
> off the whole poem into lines and half-lines (with
> tolerable correctness and only a few omissions) by the

use of capital letters, paragraph-marks, and metrical
dots or periods; and I may observe that he clearly
regarded the metre as consisting of *long* lines, not
short ones.   (EETS OS 44, p.ix).

This account of the format requires brief expansion. The
Vernon scribe does not use paragraph marks or capital letters
to signal the a-verse, for neither occurs at the beginning of
most a-verses; he does take care, however, when they occur
(except for capital letters indicating proper nouns or the
first person singular nominative pronoun, which is always
followed by a *punctus*), that they should occur at the beginning of an a-verse rather than that of a b-verse. The
punctuation, by contrast, marks off a staple half-line unit,
and although the *punctus elevatus* is used as an occasional
variant in place of the *punctus*, there is no attempt to
distinguish between a-verse and b-verse by means of
punctuation marks. In a total of eighteen cases, the scribe
has failed to punctuate what Skeat saw as the caesura of a
long line, and, if only in conjunction with the otherwise
less than conclusive evidence of capital letters and paragraph
marks, this oversight might be taken as a sign that underlying
the Vernon text, either as its immediate source or archetype,
was a long line verse format.

What this fails to explain is the scribe's or director's
original decision about format and punctuation, which makes
an obvious distinction between *Joseph* and *Piers Plowman*. It
is possible, of course, that the Vernon scribe merely copied
his exemplar for *Joseph* and reproduced its format; but this
does no more than transfer the problem to an earlier stage
in textual transmission. In discussing decisions made by the
Vernon scribe or director about the format of *Joseph*, I
should be taken to refer to the Vernon text or its exemplar.
It is also conceivable that the scribe reverted to an older
prose format for copying a verse exemplar of *Joseph* because
of shortage of space. Given the sheer scale of Vernon this
may seem improbable, but *Joseph* is placed close to the end
both of part 4 of the manuscript and of a quire: if the
manuscript was originally written in separate fascicules, as
unoriginal folio numeration from the end of part 4 and loss
of leaves from the beginning of part 5 might imply, this
could have been a determining factor.[23] On the other hand,
the scribe completes the quire with almost a whole folio to
spare, and there is no comparable cramping or breakdown in
ordinatio elsewhere in the manuscript. Moreover, the Vernon
scribe or director shows consistent care in *ordinatio*, in

grouping works depending on their suitability to two or three
columns and the application throughout of various punctuation
systems to works of different forms. "Copyists of Middle
English works (and perhaps their authors) tend to fall into
one of two classes in respect of punctuation: those
seemingly indifferent to it and those for whom it was
meaningful; and though the latter did not necessarily repeat
precisely what was in their originals, if any, they were more
likely to grasp and carry out its principles."[24] Without
doubt the Vernon scribe belonged with those for whom
punctuation was meaningful. His metrical discriminations, of
the long *SEL* line, the *Piers Plowman* line (both with
medial caesura), of tail-rhyme and short line verse, are
standard and correct. In some of the shorter poems composed
in loose alexandrine or septenary, he has decided upon a
half-line verse format where Horstmann and Furnivall opted
for a long line with medial caesura, but this is no more
than a genuine difference of editorial opinion. Vernon
uniformly maintains stanza forms in strophic poetry, even in
the complex thirteen-line stanzas of *Susannah*. For prose
items, different punctuation systems are used depending on
the rhythmicality of a particular treatise: the punctuation
used for Rolle, for example, is heavier and more regular than
that used for Hilton. One of the Vernon texts, *A Talking of
the Love of God*, draws attention in its introduction to the
need for correct punctuation;[25] and whatever the problems of
decoding the system employed and differences between the
Vernon and Simeon copies, the Vernon scribe shows a particular
sensitivity to the unusual punctuation demands of the treatise.
All the evidence is that Vernon decisions about format and
punctuation should be treated with respect.

It seems, then, that the scribe or his director wished
to distinguish meaningfully between the form of *Piers Plowman*
and that of *Joseph of Arimathea*. There is little to encourage
speculation that the Vernon text of *Joseph* is a considerable
abbreviation of an English copy,[26] and the inference must be
that the scribe or his director did not regard *Joseph* as an
alliterative poem but as some other kind of composition.

Prose format for alliterative verse copies would have
been unusual by 1400, although it was of course the normal
scribal presentation of Old English verse and the habit
survives in the two thirteenth century manuscripts of
Laȝamon's *Brut*. For texts of the new type of unrhymed
alliterative poetry in and after the second half of the
fourteenth century, there is a scribal consensus on a

different format: the long line verse format, often with
pointing of the medial caesura, originally used in English
texts for the loose alexandrine/septenary of the *SEL* and
itself an adaptation of the system for copying Anglo-Norman
laisses as well as Latin poems. It may be no accident that
two of the earliest extant manuscripts of the 'Alliterative
Revival' - King's College Cambridge MS 13 (*William of Palerne*)
and Vernon itself - also contain texts of the *SEL*.[27] This
format is standard: only one manuscript of what is beyond
doubt an alliterative poem, Bodleian MS Digby 102 of *Piers
Plowman*, uses a prose format (with careful punctuation much
like that of the Vernon *Joseph*). In view of the monastic
provenance of this manuscript,[28] it may be a sufficient
explanation that the scribe was interested not in the meter
of *Piers Plowman* but its content, and decided to present the
text for reading in a format like that of other elevated
(prose) didactic and devotional treatises. There are other
examples of prose format used in the cases of texts which are
obviously important in determining "alliterative modes and
affiliations" but by any of the standard metrical tests
cannot be classified as alliterative poems: this is true of
the *Jack Upland* group,[29] and all manuscripts of Richard
Rolle's heavily cadenced English composition, including
Vernon. In the case of Rolle manuscripts, scribes do not
regard it as necessary to interrupt their prose format even
where the text explicitly signals the beginning of a rhymed
poem:

> Þou mai3t in þi languischyng. Syngen þis in þyn
> herte to þi louerd Ihesu. whon þou coueytest his
> comyng. and þi goyng. Whon wolt þou comen to cumforte
> me. and bringe me out of care. And 3iue þe to me.
> þat i. may seo⁏ and han for euermare.
> (Vernon folio 336ʳ, column b).

No scribe or reader schooled in traditions of late medieval
Latin *Reimprosa* would have been at all perplexed by such a
continuity of format, and the punctuation systems used in
texts of the *ars rithmica* were highly sophisticated. The
Vernon text of *A Talking of the Love of God* is no isolated
exception. This evidence testifies to scribal discrimination,
not its lack, and the use of prose format for texts such as
Jack Upland or the York Register manuscript of *Gaytryge's
Sermon* should not be lightly set aside by scholars who argue
that these are really alliterative verse compositions. But
whatever caution we may feel in the face of one deviant *Piers
Plowman* manuscript can be set aside in considering the Vernon

copy of *Joseph*, for the scribe everywhere else demonstrates a level of at least normal expertise in the standard systems, using the rhythmical for Rolle and the verse for *Piers Plowman*.

The rhythmical system tends to be less uniform from one manuscript to another than the verse format, because it uses more punctuation. While much of the pointing has to do with rhythmical cadence, some is inserted (as normal in prose format) to clarify confusibles. The absence by and large of such extra punctuation in *Joseph* is therefore noteworthy, and it is enough to distinguish the system used for this text from any used for prose and/or rhythmical composition elsewhere in Vernon. There is only one text that exhibits a nearly identical system, the *Life of Adam and Eve*. There is good reason to suppose that the version of this text in Vernon is a prose rendering of a verse original, and the punctuation divides it, in effect, into short lines. In this extract I have rearranged the prose format:

> Wel fayre he departed.
> þe derke from þe liht.
> ⁋ Liht he cleped þe day.
> and þe derknesse þe niht.
> Of Euen and of morewen.
> he made a day.
> and seþþen oþur þing.
> as I wol ȝow tellen.   (folio 392^v).

(There is an evident substitution of *tellen* for *seie* in the last line, to conceal the rhyme.) The original of the piece was probably a long line poem. This observation is convincingly supported by Dr. Mabel Day's rearrangement of one passage:

> "So þat Jhesu Crist þi penaunce haþ vnderfonge(n),
> For þou wold so bleþliche dwelle þerin so longe.
> I am set to bringe ȝow þer ȝe schul haue mete,
> Such as in paradys ȝe weore wont to haue and eete(n)."
> Þe corsud angel nom Eue vp bi þe hond
> and ladde hire ... to dryue londe;
> As soone as Eue comen vp of þe water was,
> Hire bodi ... was grene as eni gras.[30]

This example is unusual, a case in which inflexible modern distinctions between prose and verse are appropriate: for it shows the Vernon scribe, or his exemplar, using a

punctuation system similar to that used for *Joseph* when
transposing an item from one mode to another. On this
analogy, the editorial process in Vernon could have removed
much of the alliteration from *Joseph*, just as rhyme is
removed from *Adam and Eve*; and the Vernon copy of *Joseph*
would then be a prototype of Malory's treatment of the *Morte
Arthure*, or even of Caxton's more rigorous erasure of
alliterative verse indications in Malory's Book V. It must
be objected that Caxton had a reason for reducing the
alliteration in Malory; to his more modern taste, the
alliterative collocations and syntax wore an uncouth
aspect.[31] The Vernon scribe or director, by contrast, is not
antipathetic to alliterative poetry; otherwise he would
hardly have copied *Piers Plowman*. Moreover, alliterative
patterns would hardly have constituted an embarrassment of
the order of predictably recurring rhyme in the presentation
of a 'prose' *Adam and Eve*; and their regular and sustained
use is licensed by Rolle's cadenced composition. The Vernon
copy may possibly have removed a little of the alliteration
from its original, but I hope to demonstrate that the
hypothesis of large-scale editorial change to the form of the
original is untenable. There is no good reason to postulate
editorial intervention that might have transposed unrhymed
alliterative verse into prose. Given my conviction that the
distinction made in Vernon between the form of *Joseph* and
Piers Plowman is meaningful, I can see only two acceptable
explanations, and they do not necessarily conflict. Firstly,
Joseph defies over-rigid modern categories of 'verse' and
'prose' and is a median form of rhythmical composition; this,
I think, is what the scribal format implies. Secondly,
although the Vernon scribe or director did not intend *Joseph*
to be read as an alliterative poem, its author may originally
have intended the opposite.

THE ALLITERATIVE QUESTION: STYLE, DATE AND DIALECT

In spite of apparent difficulties, there is much to
support Skeat's case for seeing *Joseph* as an unrhymed
alliterative poem, especially in the work's syntax and the
degree of alliteration employed.

J.P. Oakden provided a metrical analysis of *Joseph*'s 709
long lines, of which there follows a (slightly simplified)
version:[32]

1.	*aa/ax*	64	lines
	aa/xa	27	
2.	*aa/aa*	21	
3.	*aaa/ax*	3	
	aaa/xa	5	
	xa/aaa	1	
	aaa/aa	3	
4.	*ax/aa*	26	
	xa/aa	9	
5.	*ax/ax*	115	
	xa/xa	62	
	ax/xa	55	
	xa/ax	116	
6.	*aa/bb*	9	
7.	*ab/ab*	17	
8.	*ab/ba*	17	
9.	*aa/xx*	24	
	xx/aa	14	
10.	*abb/a*	2	
	aab/ba	1	
	a/bba	1	
	aab/b	3	
11.	No alliteration	113	

I have conducted my own analysis and find that my results differ a little from Oakden's. In order to arrive at a figure of 64 *aa/ax* lines, I find that Oakden must have accepted a wide divergence between alliteration and phrasal stress, raising in some cases normally unstressed elements such as pronouns and prepositions to the stressed position. This is an occasional license of Middle English alliterative poetry, but even taking the possibility into account I can find no more than 50 lines that I would confidently scan *aa/ax*. On similar grounds, in Oakden's large group 5 - verses which alliterate with each other on one element only - I would discount about 15 examples as having no alliteration whatever. The numbers in group 5 therefore remain static, and group 11 goes up to 128 or so. I should add that these few disputed lines are genuinely problematic.

What is the significance of these figures? It is that out of 709 lines, 186 (26%) alliterate in one way or other on three or more syllables, among which 50 or so, 7% of the whole, are *aa/ax*. 128 lines, 18%, do not alliterate at all, and a further 47 or so lines alliterate only within the verses. About 348 lines, just under half the total, alliterate only on one element in each verse. At the least these figures do not contradict the implicit judgment of the Vernon director that *Joseph* is not an alliterative poem in the sense that *Piers Plowman* is.

The important factor is the low incidence of *aa/ax* lines which even on Oakden's more generous count form only 9% of the total. In this respect *Joseph* resembles only *Cheuelere Assigne* (12.2%) in Oakden's tabulation of the corpus of M.E. unrhymed alliterative poetry. The divergence is crucial, for the *aa/ax* pattern is used in at least 60% of all lines of the unrhymed alliterative poems. The average on the basis of Oakden's statistics would be over 80%; and in the case of the *Destruction of Troy* (14,044 lines) the figure for *aa/ax* lines is at least 95%. This uniformity of preference for the pattern is the single most compelling reason for the description of these unrhymed poems as a corpus. The pattern occurred in Old English verse, and was perhaps the most common alliterative pattern, but no alliterative pattern in Old English verse is so statistically preponderant that it occurs in a majority of the lines of any classic poem. In critical terms, the *aa/ax* pattern may be seen as a compromise between the least alliteration necessary to bind hemistichs (*ax/ax*, *ax/xa*, *xa/xa*, *xa/ax*) and the more heavily alliterative variants commonly found in stanzaic alliterative poems (for example, *aaa/aa*, where alliteration and stress are certain to coincide only on the final stave, the rhyme). Since I distrust the validity of absolute distinctions between structural and ornamental alliteration, I am left with only empirical grounds for determining the corpus of Middle English unrhymed alliterative poetry. I can see only two safe criteria: structural alliteration confirmed as such by its conformity over all to the *aa/ax* staple pattern, and the absence of rhyme. Mere quantity of alliteration is a positive characteristic but it does not necessarily guarantee the classification of works as alliterative poems. If this were otherwise we might have to regard the Katherine Group as a collection of alliterative poems. Conformity to the *aa/ax* pattern is crucial; and both *Joseph* and *Cheuelere Assigne*, in the state of the unique text of each that we have received, fail signally to conform to this pattern.[33]

In short, *Joseph* sits oddly in Oakden's tabulation of alliterative patterns. No alliterative poems other than *Joseph* and *Cheuelere Assigne* have less than 61.1% *aa/ax* patterning, and since the latter has 12.2%, *Joseph* is the least regular member of the alliterative verse corpus as

constituted by Oakden. The *aa/ax* standard alone allows us to
define a corpus. And the corpus exists: it will not suffice
to deplore scholarly over-concentration on the *aa/ax*
pattern,[34] for we do not gain in orientation by ignoring
obvious landmarks.

Yet to say that *Joseph* is not an alliterative poem
because it fails to conform to the *aa/ax* pattern would in
itself be little more than semantic play. Is it some other
kind of alliterative poem? After all, it makes extensive
use of what must be classified as structural alliteration in
the sense that in most of the lines the alliteration
coincides with the rhythm. One attempt to reconcile this
with the work's obviously deviant characteristics and lexical
austerity is the suggestion that *Joseph* is an early poem:
the Alliterative Revival in the making. Skeat argued for a
date c.1340 on the grounds that the metre is more 'rugged'
than that of *William of Palerne*, and that there is an
inevitable law of progress in alliterative verse composition
from the rugged to the smooth.[35] This evolutionary optimism
is echoed by Oakden, who also commented on the work's
rhythmical "irregularity" (I, 167), and it has recently been
re-echoed by Thorlac Turville-Petre who wishes to date the
work before the middle of the fourteenth century on stylistic
grounds.[36] Evolutionary terminology is profoundly misleading.
It imposes an alliterative verse straitjacket on works that
are related to alliterative verse composition but only, to
mix a metaphor, by marriage. Hence works written when the
'Alliterative Revival' was in full activity have been branded,
anachronistically, as degenerate: for example, *Gaytryge's
Sermon* from the beginning of the revival and *Friar Daw's Reply*
from its close.[37] Furthermore, dating on stylistic grounds
is subjective and dangerous: the only tool we possess for
dating *Joseph* is a *terminus ad quem*, the date of the Vernon
manuscript.

To examine the form of *Joseph of Arimathea* is in fact to
discuss in microcosm "the origins of the alliterative
revival";[38] and the contents of Vernon provide us with most
of the necessary material: as well as alliterative verse
itself, both rhymed poetry (heavily alliterated lyrics, the
long lines of the *SEL*) and the often heavily alliterated
rhythmical composition of, for example, Rolle. The latter
would seem to be the most relevant influence. In examining
the problem generally, Professor Blake lays most emphasis on
the native prose traditions of "rhythmical alliteration";
while I have stressed the influence of non-vernacular models,

especially the *ars dictaminis* and the *ars rithmica*, on
rhythmical formalization. There is agreement, however, that
the boundaries between prose and alliterative verse in the
fourteenth century and earlier were fluid, and the vital
point is well made by Professor Salter: "we have certainly
no guarantee that the process we are trying to recover always
operated as a diffusion of verse into looser prose formats."[39]
I think it probable that the original form of *Joseph of
Arimathea* stood where today we might wish to draw the boundary
between verse and prose. In the present state of knowledge
to say more than this may be to make historically invalid
distinctions. If the date is early, say 1330-50, *Joseph* is an
important text in that it would represent a movement in
English composition towards an approximate form of unrhymed
alliterative verse. If the date is later, as I think on
balance is more probable, *Joseph* may instead show the
influence of unrhymed alliterative verse on other forms of
English composition. I feel that this may well be the
distinction indicated by the scribal system; but given our
ignorance about the date of the original, there is no room
for certainty.

It remains to present an assessment, which need occupy
little space, of the degree of *Joseph*'s affinity to the *aa/ax*
poems. The diction of *Joseph* is more spare and prosaic than
that of any *aa/ax* poem, including *Piers Plowman*; in this it
is rivalled again only by *Cheuelere Assigne* in the unrhymed
alliterative verse corpus as constituted by Oakden. There
are no alliterative compound nouns in the work, and very few
words that Oakden classifies as exclusively or chiefly
alliterative. Most of these fall into the class of "chiefly
alliterative," and most are Northern dialect forms such as
carpen or the small number that the work employs of the
possible range of alliterative synonyms for 'man': *burne,
gome, schalk*. Of the two or three exclusively alliterative
forms, þro*ly* , for example, appears in *Piers Plowman*, which
is not a work of consciously elevated diction. One word
alone has a high and formal alliterative pedigree: the verb
fils(t)nen (line 618), for which MED records the only other
uses in the poems of Cotton Nero A x and *St. Erkenwald*. There
is a handful of possible archaisms, all recorded in the
glossary, and a handful of rarer words of Norse derivation
and a limited poetic life of which the verb *witer* (466) and
the adjective *greiþli* (88) are most striking. The noun
blusch drew Oakden's special attention as "exclusively
alliterative," but the phrase in which it occurs, 'þe *furste
blusch*' (657) was probably then as now idiomatic (*MED blish*,

n, sense 2). Nor is the syntax of *Joseph* complex in construction, although it imitates modestly some of the features of the word-order of *aa/ax* poems such as inversion and a preference for placing main verbs in the a-verse and relative clauses in the b, along with occasional line-fillers such as *trewely forsoþe* (line 3). Skeat noted a resemblance between the diction of *Joseph* and *William of Palerne*, but he edited these texts early in his career: while it is true that many of the words in *Joseph* also occur in *William of Palerne*, the resemblance is not remarkable and the vocabulary of *William of Palerne* is a good deal more extensive than that of *Joseph* (even relatively ornate).[40] This evidence does not altogether rule out the possibility that *Joseph* is an early work showing a stage in transition from prose or rhythmical composition to *aa/ax* poetry proper; but the probability, especially in view of the fact that the few remarkably alliterative words in *Joseph* are given their currency by the *aa/ax* poems themselves, is that (as it stands in Vernon) *Joseph* shows some influence from the newer alliterative poetry in a less than wholehearted imitation of some of its peculiarities.

This conclusion has a negative implication for study of the work's dialect, since many of the Northern features remarked in the poem seem to me to fall into the category of borrowings from formal alliterative poetry; they are at least arguably a matter of style, not of dialect. These Northern features are discussed by Skeat (pp.x-xiv) and by Oakden (I, 58-61), who reach contrary conclusions and do not appreciate the stylistic complications of the evidence. Moreover, the work of Professors McIntosh and Samuels has invalidated the kinds of analysis which led to such conclusions; and until the publication of the much-needed Edinburgh Survey scholars in the Middle English field will continue to lack the means of replacing outmoded tools. Professor Samuels has identified the dialect of the Vernon scribe as belonging to North Worcestershire.[41] I am unable to penetrate beyond the scribal dialect, and I cannot see that at present any definitive statement about the dialect of *Joseph* can be offered.

To return to questions of style: as nearly all commentators on the poem have observed, the author of *Joseph* demonstrates greatest artistry in his quite free rendering of a long battle sequence in his source (489-614).[42] This is achieved by means on the whole of fairly standard lexis (*hache, helme, stiffest, strengþe, braynes, breek* and so on) and some stereotyped recurrent collocations. For example, permutations on two alliterative collocations open the first four of the six manuscript paragraphs of folio 404ʳ:

Þe kyng boskes lettres anon . to bounen his bernes (413).

Þane he buskes touward þe bente . þer þis oþer byden (450).

Þe kyng Boskes lettres anon . to boune mo bernes (472).

Now þei bouwe touward þe bente . þer þis oþere houen (489).

These lines are repetitively formulaic in a manner resembling Laȝamon's stock recurrent phrases rather than the collocational procedure of fourteenth century *aa/ax* poetry. The analogy with Laȝamon, however, should not be pressed, especially since in general Laȝamon economically deploys his evocations of Old English heroic poetry to sketch in an atmosphere of inspiring carnage, and tends to revert to his barer rhymed lines for the details of an action. In investigating the battle sequences in *Joseph* I have examined all relevant *aa/ax* poems, especially *Morte Arthure, Alexander A*, the *Destruction of Troy* and *William of Palerne* as well as prose and rhymed romances including Chaucer's *Knight's Tale*. To be sure, I have found occasional phrasal parallels in other works: but it is not at all clear what status such evidence might claim. Most of the phrases are not inflexible but systemic: substitution in at least one element from poem to poem and within the same poem is common. The problem is particularly acute when the results show affinities with poems in more than one form: the battle sequences in *Joseph* have arguably as much in common with those in *Partonope, Ipomedon*, the *Battle of Otterburn* or the *Knight's Tale* as with any *aa/ax* poem. I have formed two preliminary judgments from my *ad hoc* survey: that the war sequences in Middle English poetry vary much more considerably within individual works and from work to work than the often battle-fatigued reader might think; and that the poetic battle-sequences in whatever metrical form are closer to one another than to any prose sequences.[43] There is a good case for believing that Middle English poets of all types felt a decorum in linking war descriptions with the effect of insistent alliteration (which Skeat, after all, romantically compared to "the rapidity and impetuosity of a charge of cavalry, and a sound as of the galloping of horses").[44] If this is so, the fact that the most convincing alliterative writing in *Joseph* occurs in battle sequences does not strengthen a case for it as a full-blooded alliterative poem. I am impressed most of all, however, by the need for a thorough and systematic analysis of battle language in Old and Middle English writings of all kinds in terms of lexical and structural patterns, and with attention to sources and contemporary treatises on warfare. At present I can do no more than report that I hope to undertake such a study.

On a few occasions an editor committed to conjectural emendations on metrical grounds (which I am not) could be tempted to 'restore' alliteration. In line 325, for example,

> when þei comen to þe halle   þei maden þe signe,

the emendation [*sale*] for *halle* would at least bind the verses. Similarly, in lines 450 and 489 (quoted above, p.xxi), a regular aa/ax line could easily be produced by normal poetic inversion of subject and verb in 450b and by this, together with substitution of [*byden*] for *houen*, in 489b. One could improve the alliteration of line 176,

> As he lai at niht keuered in bedde

by simply substituting [*the kyng*] for *he*: the source reads, in the shorter version, "Au soir quant *li rois* eualac se fu couchies en son lit."[45] However, there is little license for such emendation given the number of lines devoid of alliteration yet demonstrably close translation. Although the Vernon copy of *Joseph* may conceivably be an abbreviated edition of an original English work, the indications are that the *form* of the original has not been subjected to drastic tampering.

It seems to me probable that *Joseph* is in fact a half-alliterated poem, a first draft of an alliterative poem in the process of being written, awaiting revision and alliterative embellishment. The Vernon scribe could then be judged to have done his best with an unrevised copy perhaps made to order for Vernon itself for the reason I have suggested, interest in Joseph of Arimathea. This cannot be established beyond doubt, but there is much to commend it, especially since alliteration fails most dramatically in passages of drastic précis (below, *The Source*), and the alterations to the French source consistently emphasize the importance of Joseph at the expense of his son. There is no objection to the theory on grounds of date or dialect, and it must stand as the most cogent explanation of the state of

the text and the scribe's reluctance to present it in
standard alliterative verse format. Perhaps like *Cheuelere
Assigne*, which is also a drastic epitome of its source,
Joseph of Arimathea is not the 'Alliterative Revival', but an
alliterative poem,in the making. It is a frame of rhythmical
composition lacking the finish of meter.

THE SOURCE

Joseph of Arimathea enters the burgeoning French
vernacular Arthurian cycle shortly after Chrétien de Troyes
penned the first French references to the Holy Grail.[46]
Around the year 1200 Robert de Boron produced his verse
Joseph d'Arimathie, which was very soon rendered into prose.[47]
Boron was aware of the identification of the "vaus d'Auaron"
with Glastonbury, clinched in 1191 by the discovery there of
'Arthur's tomb', and some eminent scholars have advanced the
claim that Robert somehow worked from a Latin source at
Glastonbury which recorded Joseph's protevangelization of
England.[48] This is improbable: Joseph was a late addition
to the Glastonbury propaganda (see below, *Joseph of Arimathea
in England*). In his work Boron inventively combined the
Grail - seen as both relic of Christ and vessel of grace -
with Joseph, whom he cast as a soldier of Pilate, Veronica
and her miraculous cure of Vespasian which led to the
destruction of Jerusalem. This is a development of material
drawn from the apocryphal *Evangelium Nicodemi* and *Vindicta
Salvatoris*, and it supplies the Grail with an impeccable
provenance. Boron also credited Joseph with a sister Enygeus,
and her husband was Bron, a figure drawn from Welsh legend
and the prototype of the Fisher King.

Within thirty years or so, the Cistercian *Queste del
Saint Graal* had been added to the Vulgate Arthurian cycle,
and a last work, the *Estoire del Saint Graal*, was composed
soon after to provide the Arthurian Grail with an antecedent
history.[49] On theological grounds both these works supply
Joseph with a virgin son, Josephes, for the keeping of the
Grail was defined as a high order of priesthood and Boron had
not taken the precaution of making Joseph himself a celibate.
It is Josephes who leads the expedition to England, travelling
on his magic garment. Both *Queste* and *Estoire* are primarily
spiritual fables, neither secular romance nor hagiography -
the element of *merveilles* serves an earnest purpose.

This is a very simplified account, avoiding many of the awesome problems of textual scholarship which medieval French specialists have no choice but to pursue with the fervor of Grail knights. For present purposes, fortunately, it will suffice. For *Joseph of Arimathea* has been compiled from two sources, the Vulgate *Queste* and *Estoire*. The *Estoire* has been used for the body of the text, although *Joseph* "gives no more than an outline of the prose romance, 57 pages of Sommer's folio edition and 180 pages of Hucher's text in octavo being compressed" into 709 long lines.[50] The English redaction could scarcely be more condensed. The motive behind the condensation has never been identified, but it is beyond doubt that the English author has approached the *Estoire* through a key passage in the *Queste*. The passage occurs early in the *Queste* when Galahad, having joined the Round Table, first meets the supernatural White Knight who has sent him his shield, the famous red cross on a white background. Galahad asks about the shield's history, and I quote in full the majority of the White Knight's answer:

Il avint empres la Passion Jhesucrist quarante et deus anz que Joseph d'Arimacie, li gentix chevaliers qui despendi Nostre Seignor de la sainte veraie Croix, se parti de la cite de Jherusalem entre lui et grant partie de son parente. Et tant errerent, quant il se furent mis a la voie par le comandement Nostre Seignor, qu'il vindrent en la cite de Sarraz, que li rois Ewalach, qui lors estoit sarrazins, tenoit. Et a cel tens que Joseph vint a Sarraz avoit Ewalach guerre a un sien voisin, riche roi et puissant, qui marchissoit a sa terre; et estoit icil rois apelez Tholomers. Et quant Ewalach se fu aprestez por aler sor Tholomer, qui sa terre li demandoit, Josephes li filz Joseph dist que, se il aloit en la bataille si desconseilliez com il estoit, il seroit desconfiz et honiz par son anemi. "Et que m'en loez vos?" fet Ewalach. - "Ce vos dirai je bien," fet il. Lors li comence a trere les poinz de la novele Loi et la verite de l'evangile et del crucefiement Nostre Seignor, et del resuscitement li dist il la verite, et le fist aporter un escu ou il fist une croiz de cendal et li dist: "Rois Ewalach, or te mostrerai apertement coment tu porras conoistre la force et la vertu del verai Crucefie. Il est voirs que Tholomers li fuitis avra seignorie trois jors et trois nuiz sor toi et tant fera qu'il te menra a poor de mort. Mes quant tu ne cuideras pas que tu en puisses eschaper, lors descoevre la croiz et di: 'Biau sire Diex, de cui mort je port

le signe, gitez moi de cest peril et conduisiez sain et
sauf a recevoir vostre foi et vostre creance.'"
   A tant s'en parti li rois et ala a ost sor Tholomer.
Et il li avint tot einsi com Josephes li dist. Et quant
il se vit en tel peril que il cuidoit veraiement morir,
il descovri son escu et vit ou mileu un home crucefie
qui toz estoit sanglenz. Si dist les paroles que
Josephes li ot enseigniees, dont il ot victoire et honor
et fu gitez des mains a ses anemis et vint au desus de
Tholomer et de toz ses homes. Et quant il fu venuz a
sa cite de Sarras, si dist a tout le pueple la verite
que il ot trovee en Josephe et manifesta tant l'estre
del Crucefie que Nasciens recut baptesme. Et en ce
qu'il le crestiennoient avint que uns hons passoit par
devant aux, qui avoit le poing coupe et portoit son
poing en l'autre main. Et Josephes l'apela a soi et cil
i vint; et si tost com il ot touchie a la croiz qui en
l'escu estoit, si se trova cil gariz dou poing qu'il
avoit perdu. Et encor en avint il une aventure molt
merveilleuse. Car la croiz qui en l'escu estoit s'en
parti et s'aerdi au braz de celui en tel maniere que
puis ne fut veue en l'escu. Lors recut Ewalach baptesme
et devint serjanz Jhesucrist, et ot puis Jhesucrist en
grant amor et en grant reverence et fist garder l'escu
molt chierement.
   Apres avint, quant Josephes se fu partiz de Sarras
entre lui et son pere et il furent venu en la Grant
Bretaingne, qu'il troverent un roi fellon et cruel qui
ambedeus les emprisonna et avec els grant partie de
crestiens. Quant Josephes fu emprisonnez, tost en ala
loing la novele, car alors n'avoit home ou monde de
greignor renommee, et tant que li rois Mordrains en oi
parler. Si semonst ses homes et ses genz entre lui et
Nascien son serorge et s'en vindrent en la Grant
Bretaigne sor celui qui Josephe tenoit en prison; et le
deseriterent tout et confondirent toz cels dou pais,
si que en la terre fu espandue sainte crestientez.[51]

The most famous English translation of this passage is
of course Malory's. It merits quotation here, especially
because Malory agrees with the author of *Joseph* in further
specifying the doctrinal content of Josephes' homilies to
Evalac as the Trinity:

   'Syr,' seyde the knyght, 'hit befelle aftir the
   Passion of oure Lorde Jesu Cryste two and thirty yere
   that Joseph of Aramathy, that jantyll knyght the whych

toke downe our Lorde of the holy Crosse, at that tyme
he departed frome Jerusalem with a grete party of hys
kynrede with hym. And so he labourde tyll they com to
a cite whych hyght Sarras. And that same owre that
Joseph com to Sarras, there was a kynge that hyght
Evelake that had grete warre ayenst the Sarazens, and
in especiall ayenste one Sarezyn the whych was kynge
Evelakes cousyn, a ryche kynge and a myghty, whych
marched nyghe hys londe, and hys name was called
Tholome la Feyntis. So on a day thes two mette to do
batayle.

'Than Joseph, the sonne of Aramathy, wente to kyng
Evelake and tolde hym he sholde be discomfite and slayne
but he leffte hys beleve of the olde law and beleeve
uppon the new law. And anone he shewed hym the ryght
beleve of the Holy Trynyte, for the whyche he agreed
unto with all hys herte.

'And there thys shylde was made for kynge Evelake in
the name of Hym that dyed on the Crosse. And than thorow
hys goodly belyeve he had the bettir of kynge Tholome.
For whan kynge Evelake was in the batayle there was a
clothe sette afore the shylde, and whan he was in the
grettist perell he lett put awey the cloth, and than hys
enemyes saw a vigoure of a man on the crosse, where-
thorow they all were discomfite.

'And so hit befelle that a man of kynge Evelakes
was s[m]ytten hys honde off, and bare that honde in hys
other honde. And Joseph called that man unto hym and
bade hym with good devocion touche the crosse. And as
sone as that man had towched the crosse with hys honde
hit was as hole as ever hit was tofore.

'Than sone afftir the[re] felle a grete mervayle,
that the crosse of the shylde at one tyme vanysshed,
that no man wyste where hit becam. And than kynge
Evelake was baptyzed, and the moste party of all the
people of that cite.

'So sone aftir Joseph wolde departe, and kynge
Evelake wolde nedys go with hym whethir he wolde or
nolde. And so by fortune they com into thys londe that
at that tyme was called Grete Bretayne, and there they
founde a grete felon paynym that put Joseph into preson.
And so by fortune that tydynges com unto a worthy man
that hyght Mondrames, and he assembled all hys people
for the grete renowne he had herde of Joseph. And so
he com into the londe of Grete Bretaygne and disheryted
thys fellon paynym, and confounded hym, and therewith
delyverde Joseph oute of preson. And after that all the
people withturned to the Crystyn feythe.[52]

xxxiii

With typical thoroughness Skeat included an earlier edition of the *Queste* passage in his introduction to *Joseph*, but without comment other than that it gives a history of the shield. It does more than this: it demonstrates why the English *Joseph* ends with an abruptness that scholars concentrating on the *Estoire* have found inexplicable:

```
700  Þenn seis Iosaphe     þat Ioseph his fader
     mot abyden him     and dwelle þer stille,
     while þat he and Naciens gon     nouþer þei nusten
     forte cristene þe folk     and casten þe false.
     But þere an vnsely kyng     in prison hem caste
705  wiþ muche serwe to himself     siker atte laste,
     for þe kyng Mordreyns     com with suche strengþe
     forte liuere hem out:     on lyue he lafte none.
     Siþen þei bitauȝten þe blod     twei burnes to holden,
     and þei lenden of þe toun     and leuen hit þere.
```

This represents an extraordinary leap across the sequence of the *Estoire*; but it adheres for the most part to the sequence of the *Queste* passage, of which lines 704 to 707 are in fact a less than normally abridged translation. It also, incidentally, proves that the English work is not unfinished. However, there is a further textual problem with this passage, discussed below (p.xxix).

The realization of this *Queste* passage's significance explains several problems. Firstly, it explains why the author of *Joseph* departs from the usual order of *Estoire* manuscripts to introduce, out of context, God's command to Joseph to father a second son, Galahad, whom the English author appears to have confused with the Grail Knight (228-33, and 230-2,n). The context of the *Queste* passage is enough to keep the name Galahad firmly in the English author's mind. Secondly, the *Queste* passage explains the essentially casual use of the *Estoire*, which is, as it were, sporadically raided in varying degrees of detail for authorial purposes not of *brevitas* but of *amplificatio*.

Thirdly, the recognition of the structural importance of the *Queste* passage explains the nature of the English author's interest in Joseph. Lines 708-9, unless they are a scribal abbreviation, show that there is no intention of proceeding through the rest of the White Knight's speech, which deals with Josephes' death, his final instructions about the shield to Evalac (whose baptismal name is Mordrain, and who is the Maimed King), and generally connect the past history of the

Grail with the Arthurian Quest. Decisively, then, the point at which the English author breaks off reveals his lack of interest in the history of the Grail and its Arthurian connection. For him, the Grail is simply a sacred object of reverence, *þat ilke blod*, and the emphasis is on its content not its form (see line 40,n). The author's interest clearly lies not in Joseph's reputation as protevangelist of England, since that is the part of the story he chooses not to tell, but in the story of the conversion of a heathen king. The only part of the story that extends to Britain (704-7, quoted above) proves the lasting efficacy of that conversion. And in this specialized genre the interests of the author of *Joseph* and the director of Vernon are as one. It is not only many of the saints' legends in Vernon that treat the topic of an evangelist's converting a pagan prince: the three homiletic romances, *Ypotis*, *Robert of Sicily*, and *The King of Tars* have this same subject-matter and are similar in structure. Similar too are the shorter pieces, the *Dispute between Jesus and the Jewish Doctors*,[53] in which the Jew is converted by, among other things, the Christian's power to call up a sight of King Arthur and the Round Table. Admittedly, the long speeches by Joseph and Josephes in the *Estoire*, which propound the theology to which Evalac finally succumbs, are drastically abridged in *Joseph*; but the author provides the essentials. Like his model in the *Queste*, the author of *Joseph* pays more attention to the fact and manner of Evalac's conversion than its doctrine. And the manner of his conversion is in the last resort miraculous: Evalac unveils his magic shield, prays to it in the words prescribed by Josephes, and in the fuller account of the *Estoire* divine help is immediately forthcoming in the invincible form of the very White Knight who gives Galahad the account in the *Queste*. It is for this reason, not from any atavistic or heroic stirrings, that the battle sequence in *Joseph* receives such relatively detailed treatment: as its author conceives of the narrative, the supernatural victory is in every sense climactic because - as Josephes and his father have foretold - it is the proof of the Word and the final instrument in Evalac's conversion. Evalac may have found the theology hard to grasp, but there is no arguing with such a practical demonstration of the divine power to intervene in human history.

Since the author's primary interest - like that of several popular romances - is in the conversion of heathen potentates, there is solid ground for conjecture that the lost beginning of the work contained at least a summary

version of Vespasian's cure and conversion by Veronica. This
is not mentioned in the *Queste* passage but the author would
have found it at the start of the narrative of the *Estoire*.
The legend would in any case have made a convenient preface
to the Joseph story, as it was Vespasian who supposedly freed
Joseph shortly before his final assault on Jerusalem;
moreover, it would have enabled the author to include in his
work not one but two conversions of pagan princes. There is
no estimating the length of the lost opening, but if the
author's treatment of the *Estoire* was as condensed as in the
extant sections it need not have been at all extensive, and
it may certainly have run to less than 100 lines. On the
other hand, the English author did not have the *Queste* to
provide a taut framework for the episode, and he may therefore
have presented a fuller than usual version of the *Estoire*,
perhaps using subsidiary sources (see 12-20,n). It may have
been the Jerusalem-based opening of *Joseph of Arimathea*,
after all, that set the Vernon director in mind of the next
item, *Judas and Pilate*.

This material presents an ampler picture of the reasons
behind Vernon's inclusion of *Joseph*. Indeed, the Vernon
director may have been so in sympathy with this shaping
generic interest in the original that he further sharpened
its outlines with a few minor omissions. It is worth noting
here that there is room for suspecting a hiatus in the Vernon
copy after line 703 (quoted above, p.xxvii). Working here
from the *Estoire*, the author has Josephes instructing his
father to await him in Sarras while he and Naciens (Seraphe)
go to convert more heathens *nouþer þei nusten*. Immediately
after this, þere in line 704a refers, in both *Estoire* and
Queste versions, to Britain; and according to both sources
Joseph went to Britain with his son. While *hem* in line 707
may refer only to Josephes and Naciens, lines 708-9 (whose
twei burnes refers to the men in whose hands, according to
the *Estoire*, Josephes left the ark when he departed from Sarras)
imply that the author is at least aware of Joseph's presence
in Britain. The probable explanation for this slight
confusion is a scribal hiatus of no more than two or three
lines of summary narrative. I hope to have established in
this discussion that the author of *Joseph* had a coherent
program, in his use of the *Queste* passage as model and in his
view of the narrative as concerning the evangelical conversion
of a pagan king. Given this reason for modest confidence in
the author, in places where the senses of the Vernon copy
seems disjointed to a considerable degree of incoherence
there may be cause to suspect either scribal abridgement or,

as I have argued, that the Vernon scribe had to make do with an unrevised first draft of the projected English work. With this in mind I now turn to the *Estoire*, which is the main source of the work's narrative detail.

The manuscripts of the *Estoire* form at least three groups: a longer, a shorter, and a mixed version. W.R.J. Barron has carefully compared different manuscripts of all three with *Joseph*, and concludes, as far as textual variants in the French and the brevity of the English permit, that the English author seems to have worked from a manuscript of the longer redaction. Properly, he warns of "the dangers involved in identifying the source of *Joseph* ... in specific texts of the *Estoire*" (p.193). Accepting Barron's findings, I have extracted citations mainly from Hucher's edition of the long redaction (*H*) although I have also consulted other available texts and editions. The English author appears to have extracted from the *Estoire* what he regarded as essential narrative elements and to have left out most of the verbal ornament. The same policy is applied to speeches: the gist of a speech, whatever justifies its place in the narrative, is extracted; and so are the narrative, rather than the abstract and dogmatic, elements within speeches. Thus Joseph's second speech to Evalac, detailing the conception and life of Christ, is a close but selective translation of the French, as is the subsequent exchange between Evalac and Joseph and Evalac's vigorous rejoinder:

> 'What, mon?' quaþ þe kyng, 'þou castest þiseluen.
> Toldest þou not now biforen   he nedde neuer fader,
> but elles withoute mon   ibore of a mayden?
> And þou seist now he has on - hou may þis sitte same?'
> (117-20)

H p.142:

> Par foi, dist Evalach, jou te tiens pour yvre, car puis que tu m'as une cose recouneue, et puis si le me noies apres. Car encor tiesmougnes-tu de ton Diu que il a piere, et si dis que il ne fu pas engenres de carnel compaignie et cou ne peut avenir. Ne raisons ne verites ne samble cou mie.

A further exchange in the source, however, is entirely omitted, and the long theological speech of Joseph's which follows it in the French (*H* 142-51) is extremely compressed and deliberately simplified in the English (121-36). The

first three lines of the English (121-3) are without
alliteration, but there is no disjuncture of sense or syntax
here to indicate scribal abbreviation. The sections of the
Estoire which receive most careful and literal translation
contain the miraculous or marvellous elements: Evalac's
dream, Josephes' vision of Christ in the ark, Josephes'
prophecy of Tholomer's invasion and the spectacular demise
of the heathen clerk. In the battle sequences, the author
shows an unusual and sustained degree of independence from
his source for the initial encounters, but reverts to closer
translation when the vital elements of the shield and the
coming of the White Knight are introduced. The closest piece
of translation in the whole work occurs within the account of
the early and secret conversion to Christianity of Evalac's
queen by a wise hermit, which provides the author with a
third conversion motif (631-62). On this occasion however he
retains only what is suitable to the main line of the
narrative, Evalac's conversion, and omits the long account of
incidental wonders consequent on the queen's meeting with the
hermit (see 661,n). As in many of the French manuscripts,
there is understandable confusion between Joseph and his son
Josephes, but, more than this, the English author plays down
the rôle of the son. There is also a policy of condensing
speeches (indeed, a long speech by Christ explaining the
symbolic significance of Josephes' vestments is cut entirely:
see 258-312,n), and, significantly, of minimizing the
portentous eucharistic themes central to the *Estoire*. More
detailed analysis is provided in the notes to this edition.

At times the author has deviated from the order of the
source to include a picturesque detail transposed from some
other part (see 313-23, n). At other times the elision of
the sequence in the source is disturbingly abrupt, and each
instance is mentioned in the notes. For the most part, there
is no good reason to doubt that the elision or transposition
is other than authorial, and in such cases the frequent
appearance of several lines without alliteration is to be
seen in the same light as 121-4 (see preceding paragraph), as
a sign of drastic authorial précis. Because of his single-
minded interest in conversion and miracles, the author's
treatment of the *Estoire* is often cavalier; the result is
sometimes inauspicious, but generally makes sense. There are
one or two bad mistranslations (see especially 458,n). In a
very few cases, however, the sense utterly breaks down and
transitions become abrupt enough to engender suspicion of
textual corruption or scribal abridgment. I have already
examined the case of þere in line 704 which, in the Vernon

copy as it stands, defeats altogether the textual function of language. The probable explanation in that instance is a scribal hiatus, and I have recorded in the notes other possible examples of scribal omission or, more likely, editorial shortening of the text in Vernon or its exemplar. I should emphasize that in all other instances I feel confident of the authorial nature of changes to the *Estoire*, which often involve intricate restructuring. Even if the few queries I have raised about possible scribal omission were correct, and in most cases they are frankly conjectural, the original text of *Joseph* would not have been much longer than it stands in the Vernon copy. There is nothing here to disturb the theory that the scribe did his best with an unrevised original, perhaps commissioned for Vernon itself.

THE TEXT

Joseph of Arimathea should be edited in a manner which conveys important features of the Vernon format. The Vernon text of *Joseph* may perhaps be a slightly shortened version of the original; but this does not affect the form of the original, merely its length. I am persuaded that the reason for the format was not shortage of space but a conviction in the Vernon workshop that *Joseph* was not, as it stands, an alliterative poem like *Piers Plowman*. In its extant state, *Joseph* is an alliterative composition which manifests some of the qualities of both poetry and prose. None the less, a verse format is more suitable than prose to modern readers, for two reasons. Firstly, the strong rhythmical formalization of the work, implied in my use of the word 'composition', is obtrusive; secondly, a readable prose format would destroy some of the significant characteristics of the Vernon system.

Skeat's answer to the problem was a reproduction in part, in long verse lines, of the Vernon punctuation (the medial *punctus* of each line marked in the text, the end stop represented by white space) and capitalization. This is valuable, but the use of a point as a symbol in both modern and medieval punctuation, and the retention of Vernon's capitalization, do not make for easy reading.

From the syntactic structure of the b-verses, capitalization, and the occasional scribal failure to mark a caesura, it is evident that the Vernon copy of *Joseph* has its basis, either as scribal exemplar or authorial intention, in long line format. I have therefore followed Skeat in adopting this format, but have indicated the caesura by a medial space. I have not treated as exceptional the few lines where the scribe has omitted or misplaced the caesura, for these are without doubt errors which I have corrected silently. The format adopted has the advantage of making possible modern punctuation and capitalization, which, together with modern word-division and paragraphing, I have employed throughout. Contractions, suspensions and abbreviations are all expanded silently. I have introduced a small number of editorial emendations, each of which is indicated by square brackets in the text and defended in the notes. A clarification of the sense of line 71 is not, I think, an emendation but a question of proper word-division.

JOSEPH OF ARIMATHEA IN ENGLAND

In assessing English interest in Joseph it is well to recognize a dichotomy between accounts which were influenced by Glastonbury propaganda and those which were not. *Joseph of Arimathea* belongs to the second category.

In the wake of Geoffrey of Monmouth's coruscating fictionalization of British history, the monks of Glastonbury inserted two new characters into their official history, the *De Antiquitate Glastoniensis Ecclesiae* written before 1135 by William of Malmesbury.[55] The two characters are Joseph of Arimathea and Arthur, neither of whom is connected with Glastonbury by William. William noted with polite scepticism a theory that the abbey was founded in the first century A.D. by disciples sent over by St. Philip who supposedly evangelized Gaul, but he preferred another version of the abbey's foundation which supplied a second century date. This notwithstanding, William upheld Glastonbury's claim to be the oldest and most important religious foundation in Britain. Yet in a revision of the history dated around 1240, the abbey has expanded this claim to include not only Arthur, whose tomb at Glastonbury had been miraculously discovered in 1191 at a time of "financial and ecclesiastical crisis", but also a "fantastic forgery"[56] of a charter of foundation, the *Charter of St. Patrick*, which accepted the story of the evangelization of Britain from Gaul in 63 A.D. and made Joseph of Arimathea the leader of the expedition. Since this detail is not mentioned in William's history, it must have been imported to Glastonbury before 1240 from some other source; and the probable source is of course Robert de Boron, with whose work the 63 A.D. date did not conflict. Professor Lagorio has traced the development from this point of the Glastonbury claim to Joseph. It is a fascinating political record of the abbey's self-interested service of the English crown at a time of ecclesiastical schism and political strife. "The promotion of a legend which linked King Arthur and Joseph, and proclaimed an apostolic conversion for Britain which well antedated the founding of the Church at Rome, would bolster England's national and ecclesiastical claims to precedence and independence" from the papacy (p.220). The Glastonbury monks were not anxious to lay claim to the Holy Grail, for the romance tradition of the Grail as super-eucharistic vessel of grace was regarded by the Church as heterodox; but two cruets containing Christ's blood made an acceptable substitute for Joseph to have brought to the abbey. The abbey of Hayles had a similar inspiration, and profitably laid claim to the blood even in the absence of the prestigious evangelist.[57] The revised Glastonbury account was authoritatively recorded in the late fourteenth century by John of Glastonbury,[58] and John serves as the model for most fifteenth and early sixteenth century English lives of Joseph: in Hardyng's *Chronicle*,[59] in de Worde's Life of *Joseph of Arimathy*, in the third edition (1516) of the *Nova Legenda Angliae*, and the somewhat enthusiastic poem published by Pynson in 1520.[60] According to Lagorio, the Glastonbury version also appears to have influenced Lovelich and perhaps Malory.[61] Even so, the third edition of the *Nova Legenda Angliae* marks the first recognition of Joseph in an English legendary, and he first appeared as a saint in the *Roman Martyrology* in 1545.

There is absolutely no sign in the Middle English *Joseph of Arimathea* of any interest in, or knowledge of, the Glastonbury account. Indeed, *Joseph* varies from it in essential aspects, not merely in altogether omitting the British content of the Grail romances crucial to the Glastonbury claim, but also in following the *Estoire*'s record of Joseph's second imprisonment in Jerusalem for a period of 42 years after Christ's Passion. This of course conflicted with the chronology of the Glastonbury claim, already fixed from early use of the St. Philip legends, William of Malmesbury's note and Robert de Boron; and so in the Glastonbury version it had to be left out. It may be tact, not a bad manuscript, which led Malory (above, p.xxv) to speak of an intermission of 32, not 42, years between the Crucifixion and Joseph's departure from Jerusalem. While the

Estoire does at least refer to Britain's conversion at the initiative of St. Philip, the author of *Joseph* chooses to omit the detail (see 7,n). Moreover, the English author does not substitute two cruets for the Grail, although in line with orthodox suspicions he respects the blood more than its container. *Joseph* therefore has no evident relation with the Glastonbury version and it is better to presume that its author had some altogether different type of interest in the saint.

His interest, I think, is literary and devotional. It is literary in that *Joseph* is one of the many Middle English translations of a romance *matière*; and it is devotional, I suggest, in that it stems from the tendency of ecstatic Marian devotion, in the often distressing visualization of the scene around Christ's cross, to honor Joseph of Arimathea as a special protector of the Virgin Mary.[62] As the other references to Joseph in the Vernon manuscript show, *Joseph* is not alone among English works in this respect. This is probably an adequate explanation too of the fact that five manuscripts of the Middle English *Gospel of Nicodemus* contain only a translation of "that part of the Gospel which is especially concerned about the life-experiences of Joseph of Arimathea."[63] The Middle English *Joseph of Arimathea* is a saint's life drawn from a quasi-historical romance, the *Estoire*, designed to elucidate a spiritual fable, the *Queste*; and the more didactic elements of the source are jettisoned for a rougher hagiographic delight in *ad hoc* miracles. A resort to the label of 'hagiographic romance', however, would do little to illuminate the nature of the work. I hope to have shown that the genre of *Joseph* is a specialized one which spans both saint's life and romance, and which determines its acceptance into Vernon along with the only three romances selected for the volume: the subject of *Joseph* is the conversion of pagan royalty. The author's response, both to the Grail story and to the legend of Joseph, is therefore idiosyncratic, and in literary terms his treatment can scarcely be judged an unqualified success, even though it has a cogent intention and modest merits, chiefly in the lively handling of dialogue. It seems to have had no English antecedents and it has no visible influence on later writing. Unlike (in its author's opinion) the Grail, the major interest of *Joseph of Arimathea* lies in its form not its content.

1 *Joseph of Arimathie*, ed. W.W. Skeat, EETS OS 44 (1871), hereafter referred to as Skeat.

2 The phrase is the title of an important article by Elizabeth Salter, *Neuphilologische Mitteilungen* 79 (1978), 25-35.

3 The calculation is that of George Kane, ed., *Piers Plowman: the A-Version* (London, 1960), p.17. Mary S. Serjeantson, "The Index of the Vernon Manuscript," *MLR* 32 (1937), 222-61, calculates (p.223) 69 lost folios. See also Gisela Guddat-Figge, *Catalogue of Manuscripts containing Middle English Romances* (Munich, 1976), pp.269-79, and F. Madan, H.H.E. Craster, N. Denholm-Young, *A Summary Catalogue of Western Manuscripts in the Bodleian Library at Oxford*, volume II, part II (Oxford, 1937), 789-92.

4 Of these, however, 113 form the *South English Legendary* and 114 the *Northern Homilies*. See A.I. Doyle, "The Shaping of the Vernon and Simeon Manuscripts," *Chaucer and Middle English Studies in Honour of Rossell Hope Robbins*, ed. Beryl Rowland (London, 1974), pp.328-41, hereafter referred to as Doyle.

5 *Sammlung Altenglischer Legenden*, ed. Carl Horstmann (1878; rpt. Heilbron, 1969), pp.3-97; see also Manfred Görlach, *The Textual Tradition of the South English Legendary* (Leeds, 1974), pp.102-04. The *South English Legendary* is hereafter cited as *SEL*.

6 EETS OS 117, ed. F.J. Furnivall (1901), pp.658-72; also ed. Carleton Brown, *Religious Lyrics of the Fourteenth Century*, revised by G.V. Smithers (Oxford, 1957), numbers 95-120. The lyrics are of prime importance to a study of alliterative modes in the fourteenth century.

7 See K. Sajavaara, *Middle English Translations of Robert Grosseteste's Chateau d'Amour*, Mémoires de la Société Néophilologique de Helsinki 32 (1967), 103-27.

8 *The Roule of Reclous*: for its textual relations, see Doyle, p.333, and E.J. Dobson, "The Affiliations of the Manuscripts of *Ancrene Wisse*," *English and Medieval Studies presented to J.R.R. Tolkien* (London, 1962), pp. 128-63.

9   See Hope Emily Allen, "Bodleian Vernon Manuscript," *Times Literary Supplement*, February 8, 1936, p.116.

10 See K. Sajavaara, "The Relationship of the Vernon and Simeon Manuscripts," *Neuphilologische Mitteilungen* 68 (1967), 428-40; N.S. Baugh, *A Worcestershire Miscellany* (Philadelphia, 1956), pp.19-21, 37-9; Angus McIntosh, "A New Approach to Middle English Dialectology," *English Studies* 44 (1962), 7; Doyle, pp.331-4.

11 See A.I. Doyle and M.B. Parkes, "The Production of Copies of the *Canterbury Tales* and the *Confessio Amantis* in the Early Fifteenth Century," *Medieval Scribes, Manuscripts and Libraries: Essays Presented to N.R. Ker*, ed. M.B. Parkes and Andrew G. Watson (London, 1978), pp.163-210, p.199: "... we can find no evidence for centralized, highly organized scriptoria in the metropolis and its environs at this time other than the various departments of the central administration of government, and no evidence that these scriptoria played any part - as organizations - in the copying of literary works." This conclusion rules out a lay metropolitan scriptorium; if Vernon were a metropolitan product, the scribe would presumably have been hired on an *ad hoc* commission basis. However, the nature of the texts selected for copying and the marked regional dialect of the scribe argue for a non-metropolitan origin, which strengthens the case, given the manuscript's scale and the expertise of its execution and decoration, for production in a scriptorium and monastic provenance.

12 Kane, p.17; Görlach, p.102; Serjeantson, p.222.

13 Valerie M. Lagorio, "The Evolving Legend of St. Joseph of Glastonbury," *Speculum* 46 (1971), 209-31.

14 Walter Hilton, *The Goad of Love*, ed. Clare Kirchberger (London, 1952), p.50.

15 EETS OS 98, p.293, and *Yorkshire Writers*, ed. Carl Horstmann, I (London, 1895), 257.

16 EETS OS 98, pp.297-328.

17 *The Apocryphal New Testament*, ed. and trans. M.R. James (Oxford, 1924), pp.94-146.

18 Index items 152-93, of which only 152-60 survive and are
    edited in EETS OS 98, pp.138-67.

19 Kane, p.51, citing *Piers the Plowman: A Critical Edition
    of the A-Version*, ed. Thomas A. Knott and David C. Fowler
    (Baltimore, 1952), pp.148-9.

20 Dr. Doyle's statement (p.336, n16) that *Joseph* "is written
    at first as prose before falling into metrical lines," is
    an error. The format is consistent.

21 See David A. Lawton, "Gaytryge's Sermon, *Dictamen* and
    Middle English Alliterative Poetry," *Modern Philology* 77
    (1979), 329-43. The Register, however, does not mark
    half-lines.

22 *Laȝamon's Brut*, ed. G.L. Brook and R.F. Leslie, EETS OS
    250 (1963) and 277 (1978). This edition reproduces
    manuscript punctuation and adopts a long line verse
    format.

23 For the folio numeration after folio 401^r, see Serjeantson,
    p.223. The collation of Vernon is not established, but
    part 5 of the manuscript consists of a single quire
    damaged at the beginning, and, given the loss of folio
    402, *Joseph* appears to stand at the beginning of the last
    (damaged) quire of part 4. For an analogous use of prose
    format to save space, see folio 89^v of the Hengwrt
    manuscript, reproduced in *The Canterbury Tales*, ed. Paul
    G. Ruggiers (Norman, Oklahoma, 1979), p.352, where hand C
    rectifies the omission of one stanza from the *Monk's Tale*
    (see Paleographical Introduction by A.I. Doyle and M.B.
    Parkes, pp.xliii, xlvi).

24 Doyle and Parkes, Paleographical Introduction, p.xxxviii.
    See also M.B. Parkes, "Punctuation, or Pause and Effect,"
    Medieval Eloquence, ed. J.J. Murphy (Berkeley, 1978),
    pp.127-42. On *ordinatio*, see M.B. Parkes, "The Influence
    of the Concepts of *Ordinatio* and *Compilatio* on the
    Development of the Book," *Medieval Learning and Literature:
    Essays Presented to R.W. Hunt*, ed. J.J.G. Alexander and
    M.T. Gibson (Oxford, 1976), pp.115-41.

25 "Men schal fynden lihtliche þis tretys in Cadence. After
    þe bigynninge. 3if hit beo riht poynted & Rymed in sum
    stude. To beo more louesom to hem þat hit reden": *A
    Talkyng of þe Loue of God*, ed. M.S. Westra (The Hague,

1950), p.2. See Margery M. Morgan, "A Treatise in Cadence," *MLR* 47 (1952), 56-64; and two articles by Lois K. Smedick, "Cursus in Middle English: *A Talkyng of þe Loue of God* Reconsidered," *Mediaeval Studies* 37 (1975), 387-406, and "Parallelism and Pointing in Rolle's Rhythmical Style," *Mediaeval Studies* 41 (1979), 404-67.

26   See below, *The Source*. The habit of editorial "tinkering", however, was not unknown to those involved in the production of Vernon. See, for further references, Görlach, p.103, and Doyle, p.335 and p.340, n34.   The word "tinkering" is used by B.D. Brown, ed., *Southern Passion*, EETS OS 169 (1925), p.xxvi, n, quoting Josephine D. Sutton, "Hitherto Unprinted Manuscripts of the Middle English *Ipotis*," *PMLA* 31 (1916), 114-60.

27   I discuss this in a forthcoming article, "Middle English Unrhymed Alliterative Verse and the *South English Legendary*," *English Studies* (1981).

28   See EETS OS 124 (1904), ed. J. Kail, p.ix.

29   *Jack Upland, Friar Daw's Reply and Upland's Rejoinder*, ed. P.L. Heyworth (London, 1968), and Salter, p.34n.

30   *The Wheatley Manuscript*, ed. Mabel Day, EETS OS 155 (1921), p.xxvii.

31   N.F. Blake, "Caxton and the Courtly Style," *Essays and Studies* 21 (1968), 29-45.

32   J.P. Oakden, *Alliterative Poetry in Middle English* (1930-5; 2 vols. rpt. as 1, Hamden, Connecticut, 1968), I, 185-6.

33   *Cheuelere Assigne*, ed. H.H. Gibbs (Lord Aldenham), EETS ES 6 (1868); for good apparatus and discussion of form, see Elizabeth G. Williams, *A Critical Edition of the "Cheuelere Assigne" from the Fifteenth Century Manuscript Cotton Caligula A ii*, unpublished M.A. thesis, University of London (1964), and for a discussion of its possible relation to Anglo-Norman *laisses*, Rosalind Wadsworth (Field), *Historical Romance in England: Studies in Anglo-Norman and Middle English Romance*, unpublished D.Phil. thesis, University of York, England (1972).

34 N.F. Blake, "Middle English Alliterative Revivals," *Review* 1 (1979), 210.

35 EETS OS 44, p.x, and W.W. Skeat, "An Essay on Alliterative Poetry," *Bishop Percy's Folio Manuscript*, ed. J.W. Hales and F.J. Furnivall (London, 1868), III, xi-xxxix.

36 Thorlac Turville-Petre, *The Alliterative Revival* (Cambridge, 1977), pp.23-4; Turville-Petre also localizes *Joseph* in "Gloucestershire or nearby" (p.31), but offers no evidence or reference. His source is perhaps Oakden (I, 59). Valueless linguistic evidence for an early date was put forward by Karl Luick, "Die Englische Stabreimzeile im XIV, XV und XVI Jahrhundert," *Anglia* 11 (1889), 392-443, 553-618: pp.569-72.

37 See Lawton, "Gaytryge's Sermon," p.335, and *Jack Upland*, ed. Heyworth, pp.28-9.

38 See, for example, Elizabeth Salter, "The Alliterative Revival," *Modern Philology* 64 (1966), 146-50, 233-7; Derek Pearsall, "The Origins of the Alliterative Revival," Binghamton Conference paper (1975), publication forthcoming; N.F. Blake, "Rhythmical Alliteration," *Modern Philology*, 67 (1969), 118-24.

39 Salter, "Alliterative Modes and Affiliations," p.34.

40 EETS OS 44, p.75. Skeat's edition of *William of Palerne* is EETS ES 1 (1867); see also the edition by N.T. Simms (Philadelphia, 1973).

41 M.L. Samuels, "Some Applications of Middle English Dialectology," *English Studies* 44 (1963), 81-94; see also Sajavaara, "Vernon and Simeon Manuscripts," p.438.

42 J.L.N. O'Loughlin, "The English Alliterative Romances," *Arthurian Literature in the Middle Ages: a Collaborative History*, ed. R.S. Loomis (Oxford, 1959), p.521. This volume is hereafter cited as *ALMA*.

43 This does not agree with the argument of N.F. Blake, "Chaucer and the Alliterative Romances," *Chaucer Review* 3 (1969), 163-9.

44 Skeat, "An Essay on Alliterative Poetry," pp.xxxiv-xxxv.

45 *The Vulgate Version of Arthurian Romances*, ed. H.O. Sommer, I: *L'Estoire del Saint Graal* (Washington, 1909), hereafter cited as Sommer. I have used the shorter redaction in this case for the simple reason that it is closer to the English. For reasons explained below, I have normally cited source references from the longer redaction, *Le Saint Graal*, ed. E. Hucher, 3 vols., II (Le Mans, 1874), hereafter cited as *H*.

46 The most convenient summary is that of H.H. Carter, ed., *The Portugese Book of Joseph of Arimathea* (Chapel Hill, 1967), pp.22-7. See also *ALMA* pp.206-17, 251-335.

47 William Roach, "The Modena Text of the Prose *Joseph d'Arimathie*," *Romance Philology* 9 (1956), 313-42; R. O'Gorman, "The Prose Version of Robert de Boron's *Joseph d'Arimathie*," *Romance Philology* 23 (1970), 449-61, and "The Legend of Joseph of Arimathea and the Old French Epic *Huon de Bordeaux*," *Zeitschrift für Romanische Philologie* 80 (1964), 35-42. The best edition of the verse *Joseph* is by W.A. Nitze, *Roman de l'Estoire dou Graal* (Paris, 1927).

48 See the discussion by Pierre le Gentil in *ALMA*, pp.251-62, especially pp.255-6, and that by Loomis, pp.285-6. The Glastonbury claim is vigorously advanced by, for example, Jean Marx, "*Le lai de Josephe d'Arimathie*," *Le Moyen Age* 69 (1963), 371-9, and "Robert de Boron et Glastonbury," *Le Moyen Age* 58 (1952), 71-88.

49 See the chapters in *ALMA* by Jean Frappier, pp.295-318, and Fanni Bogdanow, pp.325-35.

50 W.R.J. Barron, "*Joseph of Arimathie* and the *Estoire del Saint Graal*," *Medium Ævum* 33 (1964), 184-94 (p.185); hereafter cited as Barron.

51 *La Queste del Saint Graal*, ed. Albert Pauphilet, Les Classiques Français du Moyen Age 33 (Paris, 1949), pp. 32-3.

52 *The Works of Sir Thomas Malory*, ed. Eugène Vinaver, revised 2nd. ed. (Oxford, 1973), II, 879-80.

53 EETS OS 117, pp.479-84.

54 *ibid.*, pp.484-93, and *Sammlung*, ed. Horstmann, pp.204-8.

55 The history survives in the second version of the *De Regibus Anglorum*, ed. William Stubbs, Rolls Series, I (London, 1887). See also Joseph Armitage Robinson, *Two Glastonbury Legends: King Arthur and Joseph of Arimathea* (Cambridge, 1926), and R.F. Treharne, *The Glastonbury Legends* (London, 1967).

56 Lagorio, "Evolving Legend," pp.211, 213, citing *The Great Chartulary of Glastonbury*, ed. Dom Aelred Watkin, I (Frome, 1947), ccxxxv; see *Adami de Domerham Historia de Rebus Gestis Glastoniensibus*, ed. Thomas Hearne, I (Oxford, 1727), 1-122.

57 For the Middle English version of this legend, which is a clear plagiarism from the Joseph story, see *Altenglische Legenden*, ed. C. Horstmann (Heilbronn, 1881), pp.275-81.

58 Johannes Glastoniensis, *Chronica*, ed. Thomas Hearne (Oxford, 1726).

59 *The Chronicle of John Hardyng*, ed. Henry Ellis (London, 1812), pp.83-4.

60 All three are edited by Skeat with *Joseph* in EETS OS 44. See also *Nova Legenda Angliae*, ed. C. Horstmann (Oxford, 1901).

61 Henry Lovelich, *The History of the Holy Grail*, ed. F.J. Furnivall, EETS OS 20, 24, 28 and 30 (London, 1874-7), discussed by Lagorio, "Evolving Legend," pp.226-8, and (Malory) in "The Glastonbury Legends and the English Arthurian Grail Romances," *Neuphilologische Mitteilungen* 79 (1978), 359-66. Lagorio examines *Joseph* most closely in "The *Joseph of Arimathie*: English Hagiography in Transition," *Medievalia et Humanistica* 6 (1975), 91-101.

62 The devotional trend, of course, is Bernardine, and its presence would gain added weight were Vernon, as Sajavaara suggests, or some of its exemplars, to turn out to be of Cistercian provenance.

63 EETS ES 100, ed. W.H. Hulme (1907), p.xxxiii.

Select Bibliography

SELECT BIBLIOGRAPHY

Primary Sources

Joseph of Arimathie. Edited by W.W. Skeat. EETS OS 44 (1871). [Also contains the lives of Joseph printed by de Worde and Pynson]. (*Skeat*)

La Queste del Saint Graal. Edited by Albert Pauphilet. Paris: Les Classiques Français du Moyen Age 33, 1949.

Le Saint Graal. Edited by Eugène Hucher. 3 volumes. II. Le Mans: Monnoyer, 1874. (*H*)

L'Estoire del Saint Graal. Edited by H.O. Sommer. Volume I of *The Vulgate Version of Arthurian Romances*. Washington: Carnegie Institution, 1909. (*Sommer*)

Lovelich, Henry. *The History of the Holy Grail*. Edited by F.J. Furnivall. EETS OS 20, 24, 28, 30 (1874-7).

Secondary Sources

Barron, W.R.J. "*Joseph of Arimathie* and the *Estoire del Saint Graal*." *Medium Ævum* 33 (1964), 184-94. (*Barron*)

Blake, N.F. "Rhythmical Alliteration." *Modern Philology* 67 (1969), 118-24.

―――――― "Middle English Alliterative Revivals." *Review* 1 (1979), 205-14.

Doyle, A.I. "The Shaping of the Vernon and Simeon Manuscripts." *Chaucer and Middle English Studies in Honour of Rossell Hope Robbins*. Edited by Beryl Rowland. London: Allen and Unwin, 1974, pp.328-41. (*Doyle*)

Lagorio, Valerie M. "The Evolving Legend of St. Joseph of Glastonbury." *Speculum* 46 (1971), 209-31.

―――――――――― "The *Joseph of Arimathie*: English Hagiography in Transition." *Medievalia et Humanistica* 6 (1975), 91-101.

Lawton, David A. "Gaytryge's Sermon, *Dictamen* and Middle English Alliterative Poetry." *Modern Philology* 77 (1979), 329-43.

Loomis, R.S., editor. *Arthurian Literature in the Middle Ages: A Collaborative History*. Oxford: Clarendon Press, 1959. (*ALMA*)

McIntosh, Angus. "A New Approach to Middle English Dialectology." *English Studies* 44 (1963), 1-11.

Oakden, J.P. *Alliterative Poetry in Middle English*. I *The Dialectal and Metrical Survey*. Manchester, 1930. II *A Survey of the Traditions*. Manchester, 1935. Reprinted, 2 volumes as 1, Hamden, Connecticut: Archon Books, 1968.

Parkes, M.B. "Punctuation, or Pause and Effect." *Medieval Eloquence*. Edited by J.J. Murphy. Berkeley: University of California Press, 1978, pp.127-42.

Robinson, J.A. *Two Glastonbury Legends: King Arthur and Joseph of Arimathea*. Cambridge: Cambridge University Press, 1926.

Sajavaara, K. "The Relationship of the Vernon and Simeon Manuscripts." *Neuphilologische Mitteilungen* 68 (1967), 428-40.

Salter, Elizabeth. "The Alliterative Revival." *Modern Philology* 64 (1966), 146-50, 233-7.

_____ "Alliterative Modes and Affiliations in the Fourteenth Century." *Neuphilologische Mitteilungen* 79 (1978), 25-35.

Samuels, M.L. "Some Applications of Middle English Dialectology." *English Studies* 44 (1963), 81-94.

Serjeantson, Mary S. "The Index of the Vernon Manuscript." *Modern Language Review* 23 (1937), 223-61.

Turville-Petre, Thorlac. *The Alliterative Revival*. Cambridge: D.S. Brewer, 1977.

JOSEPH OF ARIMATHEA: The Text

'... sire', he seis,   'and Sonenday is nouwe.'
Þenne alle lauhwhen an heiȝ þat herden his wordes:
'Hit is two and fourti winter,' þei seiȝen,   'trewely
                                                   forsoþe,
siþen þou souȝtest þis put   and to prison eodest.'
'Now I þonke my lord', seide Ioseph,   'þat lente me of   5
                                                   his grace:
me þinkeþ but þreo niȝt   al þis ilke þrowe.'
Þenne Ioseph askes fontston   and is ifolwed blyue.
Þei folewen him and his wyf   and with him ful monye.
Siþen com Vaspasians   and was furst sped;
in þe nome of þe fader   Ioseph him folewede,   10
and hedde iturned to þe feyþ   fifti with himseluen.
Siþen he fette his fader with a ferde   and aȝeyn fondet
þer þei bosked hem out   þat hudden hem in huirenes,
made hem to huppe   half an hundret foote
forte seche boþem   þer þei non seiȝen.   15
Þus þei ladden þe lyf   and lengede longe,
þat luyte liked his leyk   þer as he lengede.
Feole flowen for fert   out of heore cuþþhe
into Augrippus lond,   was Heroudes eir,
þere monye lenginde weore   forlet of heore oune.   20

Þen com a vois to Ioseph   and seide him þise wordes,
biddes him and his wyf   and his sone eke
and alle þat þey mouȝten gete   and to God tornen,
gon out of Ierusalem   and prechen hise wordes
and neuer more come aȝeyn   whon þei weore enes þenne.   25
In þe morwe he was sone boun   don as he biddes:
Ioseph and his cumpanye   keueren on swiþe.
Ioseph ferde biforen   and þe flote folewede;
into þe lond of Betanye   þis buirnes nou wenden.
Þei carke for here herbarwe,   summe behynde.   30
Whon Ioseph herde þerof,   he bad hem not demayȝen:
'He þat ledes vs þis wei   vre herborwe schal wisse.'
Þei founden hit newely -   so wel weore þei neuere.
Amorwe þei weore diȝt   and don hem to ȝonge,
and come to a forest   with floures ful feire   35
þat was called Argos,   þat þe kyng ouȝte,
in þe lond of Damas;   þe cuntre was dere.
Þenne spekes a vois to Ioseph,   was Ihesu Crist
                                                   himselue:
'Iosep, marke on þe treo   and make a luytel whucche
forte do in þat ilke blod   þou berest aboute.   40
Whon þe lust speke with me   lift þe lide sone:
þou schalt fynde me redi   riȝt bi þi syde.

```
And bote þou and þi sone    me no man touche.
And, Iosep, walk in þe world    and preche myne wordes
to þe proudest men -    a parti schul þei here.              45
Þau3 þei þe of manas    melen and þe þreten,
beo þou noþing adred    for non schal þe derue.'
'Lord, I was neuer clerk -    what and I ne cunne?'
'Louse þi lippes atwynne    and let þe gost worche.
Speche, grace and vois    schul springe of þi tonge,         50
and alle turne to þi mouþ    holliche at enes.'
Þenne he wawes his fot -    þe blod he with him fonges -
and in þe nome of þe fader    forþward he weendes.

Þei ferden to a cite    faste bisyde
þat was called Sarras,    þer Sarsyns sprongen               55
erest þorw Abrahames wyf    þat wonede þerinne.
Ioseph tei3 to non hous    bote euene to þe temple.
He sei3 þe kyng þer he sat    and wuste þat he was wraþþed
and hopede he scholde him    touward God turne,
for he and þo of Egipte    han werret togedere               60
and þei discounfitede him han    and scaþet ful ofte.
Þe kyng and his baronage    a counseil bigonnen -
he wolde haue red of his folk    and fare to hem 3itte -
and þei forsaken hit han,    and he vnsauht sittes.
'Sire', seis Iosep,    'or semblaunt is feble.               65
In gret anguisse 3e ben,    þat nis not god greiþe.
Wolde 3e herkene to me,    icholde ow biheete
he þat is mi foundeor    may hit folfulle,
þat was ded on þe cros    and bou3te us so deore.
I am not worþi to seyn    moni of his werkes.'               70
'Þou schewest a symple skil,' quaþ þe kyng,    'of scute
                                            red þou semest
to speke of a ded mon -    what may he don þerate?'
'I schal sei ou,' quod Ioseph,    'and 3e wol vndurstonde.'
'Tel on', seis þe kyng,    'þi tale wol I here.'

'Þat tyme þat Augustus Cesar    was Emperour of Rome         75
þis reson bigon    þat I schal now rikenen,
whon God sende an angel    into Galile
to a cite bi nome    Nazareth icalled,
to a maiden ful meke    þat Marie was hoten,
and seide: "Blessed beo þou, flour    feirest of alle.       80
Þe holigost withinne þe    schal lenden and lihte.
Þou schalt beren a child    schal Ihesu b[e] hoten."
He chaungede cher and seide:    "Hou scholde I gon with
                                                       childe
withoute felauschupe of mon?"    He bad hire not demayen:
"Þou schalt be mayden for him    biforen and after           85
```

```
holliche, withouten wem,   wite þou forsoþe."
And heo grauntede þenne    to ben at his grace;
and sone aftur þat     gretnede þat greiþli mayde.
Whon he wolde ben iboren    at a blissful tyme,
he dude miracles feole     þat mony men seiȝen.             90
Þre kynges of þe Est     þroly þei comen,
and vche put him in hond    present ful riche.
Soone Heroudes þe kyng     herde of his burþe.
He lette sle for his sake    selli mony children:
foure þousend and seue score    was þe summe holden      95
þat weore islawe for his sake,    for certeyn hit telles.
Bote þorwȝ þe grace of himself    gete him heo ne miȝt.
His mooder ay with him fleih    forþe into Egipte.
Whon he com into þe lond,    leeue þou forsoþe,
feole temples þerinne    tulten to þe eorþe              100
for heore false ymages    þat þei on leeueden.
Do awei þi maumetes;   þei han trayed þe ofte.
Let breken hem atwo    and bren hem al to pouder.
Schaltou neuer gete grace    þorwȝ none suche goddes.'
Þenne seis þe kyng:   'My wit mai not leeue             105
þat þou ne melest wonderli    and most aȝeyn kuynde.
Hou scholde a child come forþ    withoute flescly dedes
bitwene wommon and mon?    My wit may not leeue.'
'Sire', seide Ioseph,    'þou hiȝtest me to heere
and I schal preue þe tale    þat I foretelle.           110
Whon God sat in his blisse    bosked in heuene,
he seiȝ þe peple þorw peine    passen into helle.
Also wel þe holyeste    heold þider euene
as þe moste fooles,   and þe fader þouȝte
þat hit seemede nouȝt,    and wolde his sone sende      115
forte bringe hem out þerof;    and þerfore he lihte.'
'What mon?' quaþ þe kyng,    'þou castest þiseluen.
Toldest þou not now biforen    he nedde neuer fader,
but elles withoute mon    ibore of a mayden?
And þou seist now he has on -    hou may þis sitte same?'  120
'He was fader', quod Ioseph,    'and for his sake called,
þat was gostliche his halt    ar he weore man formed.
And of two personos    sprong out þe þridde
þat was þe holigost,   as I beforen seide.
His godhede lees he nouȝt    þeiȝ he come lowe,         125
þat he nas God ay forþ    in his grete strengþe.
I sei þe fader was God    ar out was bigonnen,
made alle þing of nouȝt    þorw miht of him one,
dude þe prophetes to seye    þat hemself nuste
bote as hit com heom to mouþ    and meleden þe wordes.  130
Þe kuynde of þe moder    þat he on eorþe tok,
þat diȝede awei -   for he hit most [a]redde.
```

```
    Bote þe kuynde of his fader,    þat was þe furste kuynde,
    holliche euere he heold -    for þat diȝede neuere.
    Bote he was gostliche of fader   and fleschliche of         135
                                              moder,
    so þat he com twies forþ    and bi two kuyndes.'
    Þenne seis þe kyng:    'Þe lengore I here
    þe lesse reson I seo    in þat þat þou rikenest.
    Þou toldest furst of his fader    and of his furste
                                                   kuynde
    and þreo persones,    and alle þei ben goddes.'             140
    'Ȝe, sire, bote I pertly vndo    þat I haue þe profred,
    I am worþi muche blame -    what mai I seiȝe more?
    Þe sone, I tolde bifore,   fongede vr kuynde,
    tok flesch and blod    in a feir mayden.
    His godhede luttulde not    þeiȝ he lowe lihte              145
    þat he nas euere of o miȝt:    mensked he worþe.'
    Þe kyng fette forþ    feole of his clerkes
    to spute with Ioseph -    þat spedes hem luite.
    Ioseph tok þe holy writ   and tei for his teeme,
    and destruyede heore tale   withinne þreo wordes.           150
    Þe kyng biheold on his face    and on his limes lowore,
    sayȝ he was barefot    and bar him in herte
    he hedde iben of heiȝ blod   hedde he ben ibosket,
    and a ferli fair mon -    and witerli him rewes.
    'What hettestou?' seis þe kyng    to Iosep þenne.           155
    'Ioseph of Aramathie    is mi nome called.'
    'I schal sei þe, Ioseph,    as my wit þinkes,
    þow semest not ful good clerk    to kenne suche wordes.
    Þe tale is heiȝ in himself    þat þou of tellest;
    hit is ful þester to me    and moni a mon eke.              160
    I schal seie þe, Ioseph,    I haue to done swiþe.
    I may not wel lenge now.    Tomorwe meet me heere.
    Þow schalt haue liueraunce of in    and al þat þe neodes.
    Whon vre leyser is more,    vre lustnynge is bettre.'
    'I haue felauschupe wiþouten,' seis Ioseph,    'wel         165
                                                 aboute fifti,
    boþe wymmen and men    þat mote wiþ me inne.'
    Þe kyng lette fette hem forþ    biforen him to seo
    what leodes þei beon    and where þei weore boren:
    'I trouwe þat beo þi sone,'    bi Iosaphe he seide.
    'Ȝe sire, so he is    forsoþe, as I þe telle.'              170
    'Con he out of clergye?'    seis þe kyng þenne.
    'Leeue me forsoþe, sire,    þer liues no bettre.'
    Þe kyng lette lede hem    into toun lowe
    to a feir old court,    and innes hem þere.

    Now we leuen Ioseph    and of þe kyng carpen.               175
```

As he lai at niht   keuered in bedde,
in þreo þouȝtes he was   and þat weore þis ilke:
on for his grete folk   þat him wiþsaken hedde;
anoþur for Ioseps tale   þat wolde fayn he tornede;
þe þridde, how God scholde wiþouten wem   wonen in a   180
                                              mayden.
Þenne he seih in his chaumbre flor   þreo [treos] souht
                                              vp at enes.
Þe braunches on heiȝ weoren   alle of o lengþe,
bote þe bark of þat on   semede dimmore
þen ouþer of þe oþer two,   trouwe þou forsoþe.
Þat signede Ihesu Crist: for sake of vre kuynde   185
was nout outwiþ so cler,   bote wiþinne he was clene.
He calles on his chaumberleyn   to kennen vncouþes,
and he rises anon   and for ferd falles;
and he feres him vp   and bad him not ben ferd:
'Þer schal falle non euel   of þat is here formed.'   190
Þei lihten two torches   and to þis treos wenten.
Þei weore semeli bineoþe   (þei mihte not seo þe heiȝþe),
sprongen wiþ gret sped   of a good spice.
On vche braunche was a word   of þreo maner enkes,
'Gold' and 'Seluer' he seis,   and 'Asur' forsoþe.   195
'Þis makeþ,' quod þe wiht,   'þe marke of gold';
'and þis saues,' quaþ þat wiht,   'þe seyne of seluer;
and þis clanses,   as þe asur kennes.'
Þe kyng nuste wel forte seye   bi wit þat he hedde
wheþer þat he seȝe   was on forte sigge   200
oþer two or þreo   or what he miȝte telle.
Þe kyng was abascht   and to his bed buskes,
and his chaumberleyn so aferd   þat neih he felde
                                              iswowen.
Þenne he seiȝ a newe chaumbre-wouh   wrouȝt al of
                                              bordes,
a dore honginge þeron   haspet ful faste,   205
a child cominge þorw -   his come was nout seene -
siþen lenges a while   and aȝein lendes
wiþouten faute oþer faus   as þei fore sei[ȝ]en.
Þenne spekes a vois   and on heiȝ sigges:
'King, haue þou no ferli   of þat is heere formed,   210
for so God withouten wem   wende in a mayden.'

Now we leuen þe kyng   and of Ioseph carpen.
'A! lord,' quaþ Ioseph,   'how may þis limpe
of þis King Eualak,   þat con not vnderstonde?
Bote ȝif I turne him bi þis poynt   ar he henne passe,   215
beos he neuermore itornd,   treweli I trouwe.
Nou I beseche þe, Ihesu,   as þou art ful of ioye,

þat speke to hem of Israel   þorw Moyses speche,
and bad þei schulde leeuen   for noskunus þinge
in non oþur straunge god   bote studefast þe holde,   220
and wustest Daniel in þe put   þat he was inne iworpe
among þe leones feole   þat he no scaþe lauȝte,
and forȝaf þe Maudeleyn   mekelyche hire sunnes,
and siþen seidest to me   mi preyere scholde sitte;
þou heiȝtest holichurche   to haunsen hire strengþe   225
to hiȝen þi godhed,   hit helpes nout elles;
nou, gloriouse kyng,   graunte me mi boone.'
Þenne spekes a vois   and on heiȝ sigges:
'Ioseph, haue þou no care -   þe kyng schal sone torne.
Go þou most to þi wyf;   gete þou most nede   230
a child, Galaad schal be hoten,   þat goodnesse schal
                                                      reise,
þe auenturus of Brutayne   to haunsen and to holden.'
And he dos as he bad   and to his bed buskes.

In þe morwe he was vppe   and reises þis oþure.
Þenne hit þester bigon   and þonderde swiþe   235
þat þe graue quakede   and þei agrisen alle.
He biþenkes him þo   and to his whucche weendes,
and feole preiers he made   þat Ihesu Crist herde -
and spekes to hem   wiþ loueliche wordes:
'Iblesset be ȝe today,   alle myne leoue children.'   240
And he tolde hem of his crucifiing,   hou he cros
                                                      souȝte,
and of heore fadres bifore   þat he fond vnkuynde:
'Er þei speeken to me feire   and faynede me wiþ wordes,
bote þei hateden me   and hedden dedeyn.
Bote beo ȝe stable in oure fei   and foloweþ vre werkes,   245
for ȝe han more of þe lawe   þen prophetes hedden.
Þei nedden bote þe holy gost -   and so ȝe han eke,
and siþen bodiliche me   to ben at or wille.
I nul not fastenen on þe sone   þe fadres gultus:
I forȝiue ow clene   þe harm þat I hedde.   250
And cum þou hider, Iosaphe,   for þou art iugget clene
and art digne þerto -   þat dos me to lyke.
Ichul bitake þe today   in a good tyme
on þe hiȝeste þing   holden on eorþe,
non oþer of me   hit murili to habben   255
but elles vche mon of þe   þat takes hit aftur.'
He bad him lifte vp,   and þe lide warpes.
Þenne he seos Ihesu Crist   in a sad roode,
and his fyue angeles   þat forþwiþ him stoden
as red as þe fuir.   And he hem biholdes: 260
þat on beres in his hond   a cros of queynte hewe;

þat oþer beres in his hond   þreo blodi nayles;
þe þridde þe coroune   þat his hed keuerde;
þe feorþe þe launce   þat lemede him wiþinne;
and þe fyfte a blodi cloþ   þat he was inne ibraced   265
whon he lay after slauht   in þe sepulcre.
Þenne he falles for fere   forþwiþ þe wȝucche.
Eft he bad him rise vp;   he ros wiþ þe bone.
Þenne he sauh Ihesu Crist   istrauȝt vppon þe roode
whuche þe angel byfore   hedde in his hond,   270
and þe þreo nayles,   þat þe oþur biforen hedde,
in his honden and his feet   alle þei weore faste;
siþen stiken wiþ þe spere,   blod and watur louses;
biholdes touward hise feet,   say fro hem renne,
eornen al of red blod   romynge aboute.   275
Al priueliche his peyne   apertliche he sauh.
'Whi lengest þou,' quod Iosep   to his sone, 'so longe,
and so stille liggest   lokynde in þe whucche?'
'A, fader, touche me not   in þis ilke tyme,
for muche gostliche grace   me is here igraunted.'   280
Þenne þei loken in atte wȝucche   loueliche boþe.
Þenne þei seȝen Ihesu Crist   in þat ilke foorme
þat heo seȝen him sodeynliche   whon heo furst comen
after þe slauȝt to him   to þe sepulcre.
Þenne comen two angeles   wiþ twayles white,   285
and eiþer bar in his hond   a basyn of seluer;
oþur tweyne aftur hem   with cruetes sone,
and wasscheles wiþ haly water   with hem þei brouȝten;
and oþer two after hem   with sencers soone,
set wiþ riche stones,   and a viole of sence.   290
Þen com on, þe strengþe of God,   Gabriel ihoten,
wiþ þe riccheste sege   þat euer for seete seemes;
and oþer two after him   wiþ crois and mitre,
and oþure bouwynde after   wiþ vestimens sone.
He seiȝ an auter icloþed   wiþ cloþes ful riche.   295
Vppon þat on ende lay   þe launce and þe nayles,
and vppon þat oþer ende   þe disch wiþ þe blode,
and a vessel of gold   geynliche bitwene.
Ihesu made for to greiþe Iosaphe   in þat geyn weede,
and sacrede him to bisschop   wiþ boto his hondes,   300
and tolde him of his vestimens   what þei signefyen;
in vche cite þere he come   sacren on he scholde
wiþ þe selue oygnemens   þat he to him wrouȝte,
and anoyg[n]ten oþer kynges   þat to Crist torneden.
Ȝit he leres him more   loueliche himseluen: 305
'I beotake þe her, Iosaphe,   soules to kepe.
Ȝif eni þorw þi defaute   falle fro my riche,
at þe day of iuggement   þou beost ioyned harde.

I sei3e Ioseph þi fader   schal bodiliche hem 3eme,
and þou gostliche   nou 3emes hem boþe.   310
Wiþdrawe þe of þi vestimens   and do hem vp to holde.
Go now toward þe court   þe kyng for to turne.'

Þenne þei wenden heore wei   and to þe court 3ongen,
and al aboute þe paleys   haly water þei spreynden
for mony a wikkede gost   woned hedde þere.   315
Wiþouten, on þe paleys   as þei bi passeden,
wordes of Ebreu   weren iwriten of 3ore
and sein: 'Daniel of Babiloyne,   whon he fro batayle
                                                wente
fro Nabugodonosor,   þe kyng þat him hade,
called þis paleis Auntres   and forsoþe seide   320
þat hit scholde trewely   in sum tyme aftur
called beo þe paleis   merueilouse for werkes
þat þer scholde beo sey3en   þorw sonde of vr lord.'
Bi þat was a messager come   after þis men sone.
Whon þei comen to þe halle   þei maden þe signe   325
on hem of þe verrey cros,   and toward þe kyng eoden.
Þe kyng hedde geten him a clerk,   on of þe beste -
nou3where in heore lawe   was such anoþer holden -
to take Ioseph in his tale   3if he wrong seide.
'Þou toldest me 3usterday,' quod þe kyng,   'þou wost 330
                                    wel þiseluen,
of þise þreo persones -   and alle þei beoþ goddes -
and siþen of anoþer   wonder, forsoþe,
þat Ihesu withouten wem   won in a mayden.'
'Þat I tolde þe þo   I telle þe 3itte:
I nul forsake my word   for no maner þinge.'   335
Op stondes þis clerk   and seis him þise wordes:
'3if þise þreo persones   þat þou þe fore puttest
han bote on godhede,   þei nare not goddes alle.
3if vchon haue a godhede   igraunte bi himselue,
I seie þat on is also good   as þe þreo hole.   340
Þat on is a verrei god   I sei bi god greyþe;
þis oþer two nare none   in no maner þinge.'
He sprong in his sputison   and speek harde wordes
þat Ioseph hedde no space   while his speche laste.
Op stondes Iosaphe   and þe fader sittes,   345
speek wiþ an hei3 vois   þat al þe folk herde:
'Nou þe greteþ, Sir Euelak,   God of Israel
þorw his seruauntes mouþ,   and seye þe I wile.
Þou hast ise3e toniht   signefies summe.
Þow hast diskeuered hem   þer he nis not payet.   350
Heere þou schalt ha vengaunce,   verreyliche and sone,
þat al þi reume schal seo   þat þou wrong siggest:

```
for he þis ilke Tholomer      þat þou weore wont to hunte,
þat is kynge of Babiloyne,    hiderward he buskes.
Þreo dayes with þe niht    nou he þe schal driue,           355
siþen lacche þe atte laste    and þe þi lyf bireuen.
He, þat dorste nere ȝut       þe nouȝwhere abyde,
nou schal winne his wille  of þe     for þi wrong bileeue.'
Þenne stod vp þis clerk       and wolde eft dispuite;
þenne him þouȝte þat on    heold him bi þe tonge,           360
and he roungede an heiȝ    and rorede so harde
his eiȝen flowen out of his hed    and biforen him
                                                    fallen.
Þenne vp sturten þe folk    and wolden wiþ wepene
sle Iosep and his sone    for sake of þis oþer.
And þe kyng Eualac       cauȝte his swerd sone              365
and beo þe miht of Iubiter    he swor to hem alle
weore eny of heom so wood    heom forte founde,
he wolde felle hem feye    ar þei þenne ferden.
Þenne seis þe kyng:    'Mai þer out me helpe
forto saue me out     ȝif hit so lym[p]e?'                  370
'Ȝe, sire,' seis Iosaphe,    'to fonge þe trouþe.'
'And what trouwest þou of þis mon -    tides him hele?'
'Gos to oure maumetes    and proues heore mihtes.'
Þenne þei taken þis mon    and towen him to þe temple.
Anon þei brouȝten him forþ    biforen þe moste mayster,     375
calleþ vppon an ymage    þat Appollin hette
and wol not onswere a word    þauh þei scholde swelten.
Þenne spekes an ymage    in anoþer huirne,
þat [me] clepeþ Martis:    'Nouȝt is þat ȝe mene.
Appolin is bounden    and braset so faste                   380
he may not speke a word    for noþing alyue.'
Þenne Ioseph hente a staf    þat stod him bisyde,
strikes to þis Appolin    with a strong wille
þat his nekke tobarst    and brak al to pouder,
and þe fend of his bodi    fleyȝ to þe lufte.               385
Þenne þei leuen him þer    and goþ touward oþure.
Þe kyng bowes to his pors    him offring to beode.
'Let beo,' seis Iosaphe,    'I leeue þe beo bettre,
for and þou profre him eny    I schal do to preue
vppon sodeyne deþ    þou schalt sone dye.'                  390
'Do tel me,' seis þe kyng,    '- I haue þe muche truste -
of þis Tholomer and me    hou schal hit tyden?'
And he onsweres aȝeyn:    'I dar not wel sigge
for þis Cristene men    þat vmbe mong ȝongen.
Se ȝe not þe tweyne angeles    leden hem aboute?            395
Þat on bereþ a cros,    þat oþer a swerd kene.
Whersoeuere þei ben stad    such is heore strengþe
vre maystrie is nouȝt    in no maner þinge.'
```

Þenne seis Iosaphe: 'For us ne schalt þou wonde.
Vppon þe heiȝe trinite   I halse þe to telle.   400
Spek al þat þou const   and let þe kyng here.'
'Of newe þing þat is to come,' he seis,   'con I not
                                                          telle.'
Bi þat was a messager icome   and to þe kyng menes,
and seis him þat Tholomer   has taken of his londes.
'Þe riche cite of Nagister   nomen he has forsoþe.   405
Siþen he keueres vppon   and takes bifore clene
þe castel of Alongines,   and hiderward he ioynes
with sixti þousent,' he seide,   'of clene men of armes
and fifti þousend fotmen   þat redi beþ to fihte.
Þei han geten þat holt   for certeyn soþe: 410
þer is non in þat lond   þat schal hem wiþstonden.'
Þenne þe kyng was aferd,   I hete þe forsoþe,
leste þe tale of Iosaphe   ferede trewe.

Þe kyng boskes lettres anon   to bounen his bernes,
comaundes hem to meeten him   tymely on þe morwen   415
at þe castel of Carboye   þer he beden hade,
was fiftene myle   fro Sarras iholden
and oþer fiftene myle   fro þenne as þei leiȝen.
Þenne Ioseph takes him forþ   and seiþ him þis wordes:
'Wostou what þou do, kyng,   nou þat þou wendes?   420
Of þi comynge aȝein   const þou not telle.
Suche signe me is tauȝt   þou art of cun symple:
forsoþe, a mon was þi fader   þat couþe schon amende.
Þat tyme þat Augustes Cesar   was Emperour of Rome
þou wast lenged in þe lond   þat þat lorde ouȝtc.   425
Fourti knihtes douȝtres   he wolde haue of Fraunce
forte souwe selk werk   and sitten in his chaumbre.
For þou were a feir child   þou weore ifet to serue
twei feire maydenes,   and wiþ þis mon lengedest.
Þei heolden þe of herre blod   þen þou boren weore,   430
so þou souȝtes fro him   to þe Erl of Surye.
So þou and his sone   vppon a day seten,
and ȝe woxen vnsauȝt   and þou slouȝ him þere.
So þou come to þe kyng   þat þis kuþþe auȝte,
seidest þou were a kniht   and in his court laftest.   435
He was an old mon   weried of werre,
and þou weore a ȝong mon   in þi grete strengþe.
For þou toke his enemy   and brouȝtest him to honde,
forþi he ȝaf þe þis lond   after his lyue.
Hit is not allynge to carpe, sire kyng,   whereof we   440
                                                       co[nne].'
He takes non [hede] heereto   bote askes him of þe
                                                      sweuene

þat he mette on þe niht   and bad he scholde him telle.
'Whon þat þou comest aȝeyn,   wite þou schalt forsoþe;
þou miht haue more redi roume   my rikenyng to here.'
Ioseph takes his scheld   and schapes amiddes   445
a crois of red cloþ,   and kennes him aftur
whon his peril weore most   to Crist he scholde preyen,
for þer scholde no mon verreili   þat vigore biholden
þat he nis saaf þat dai   and his sore passed.

Þenne he buskes touward þe bente   þer þis oþer byden.   450
He arayes his riche men   and rihtes hem swiþe.
Anon Tholomers men   woxen þe biggore,
sone beeren hem abac   and brouhten hem to grounde.
And þei tornede aȝein -   þat tyme hit was non oþer.
Þei come bi Tholomers tentes,   vnhoused hem sone,   455
token holliche his stor   and awei streiȝten
þat þei come to a castel   faste besyde.
Þe kyng was gon to pleye him   bi a water brimme.
Þen com on prikynge   prest him aȝeynes.
He seide: 'My ladi þe queene   ou a lettre sende,   460
biddes ou wihtly be boun   to don as heo biddes.'
And he redes hit forþ   and fond þeron sone
þat he scholde wiþdrawe him   al awei þenne,
or elles Tholomers folk   wol taken him þere;
forþi heo wole þat he wite   and warnes him beotime.   465
'Ho has witered hire of þis   and ho has hire kenned?'
He onsweres anon: 'Sire, I not forsoþe,
bote þe two Cristene men   þat bydes ow at court
in gret counseil han ibeo -   I trouwe hit be
                                   þeraboute.'
And he telles him þenne   of the qwene sonde   470
þorw counseil of Iosaphe,   and Ihesu þei þonken.

Þe kyng boskes lettres anon   to boune mo bernes.
Bi þat þe niȝt was aweye   and þe day on þe morwe
þei hadden of newe folk   fourtene þousend.
He seiȝ vnder a wode egge,   siker bi hemseluen,   475
freschliche idiht   fyue hondred men of armes.
On vncastes his helm   and to þe kyng rydes,
and he kneuȝ him wel: he was his wyues broþer,
was icalled Seraphe,   a ȝong erl forsoþe
and a douȝti þerwiþ   in alle goode deedes.   480
He mihte neuer gete loue of þe kyng   muche ne luyte,
ne good herte of him,   and he non harm seruede.
He seide: 'My ladi þe qwene   me a lettre sende:
ȝif euere I halp hire at neode   I scholde hit now
                                   cuiþe.

And I am come to þi wille,   sire, wiþ þis knihtes.'   485
'Forsoþe,' he seis, 'Seraphe,   so þou euele ou3test.
Ofte I haue forset þe,   þat me sore forþinkes,
for euere þe kuynde wol be frend   for ou3t þat mai
                                                  bifalle.'
Now þei bouwe touward þe bente   þer þis oþere houen.
He arayes his riche men   and rihtes hem bettre   490
þat þorw him reowen no res   þat his red wrou3ten.
Þenne seis Seraphe: 'Holdes ou stille
and þenkes ou, good men,   þe gref is oure childre,
what wol bifalle þerof   and we ben confoundet.
Betere hit were douhtilyche   to di3en on or oune   495
þen wiþ schendschupe to schone   and vs abak drawe'.
Þei han geten on hem   þe lengþe of a gleyue.
Whon Seraphe sei3 þat men,   þei mi3te iseo sone
his polhache go   and proude doun pallede.
In þe þikkeste pres   he preuede his wepne,   500
breek braynes abrod,   brusede burnes,
beer bale in his hond,   bed hit aboute.
He hedde an hache vppon hei3   wiþ a gret halue,
huld hit harde wiþ teis   in his two hondes.
So he frusschede hem with   and fondede his strengþe   505
þat luyte mi3te faren him fro   and to flui3t founden.
Þere weore stedes to str[iu]en   stoures to medlen.
Meeten mi3tful men,   mallen þorw scheldes.
Harde hauberkes toborsten   and þe brest þurleden.
Schon schene vppon schaft   schalkene blode.   510
Þo þat houen vppon hors   heowen on helmes;
þo þat hulden hem on fote   hakken þorw scholdres.
Mony swou3ninge lay   þorw schindringe of scharpe,
and starf aftur þe deþ   in a schort while.
Þer weoren hedes vnhuled,   helmes vp haunset,   515
harde scheldes toclouen   on quarters fellen,
slen hors and mon   holliche at enes.
Þe stiward of Eualak   in þe stour lafte,
lai streiht on þe feld   striken to þe eorþe.
Now Eualac and Tholomer   twies han asemblet.   520
Seraphe takes of heore men   wel a two hundred
to wende to a roche   was faste bisyde.
Hedde þei geten þat holt,   for certeyne soþe,
þei mihten haue do muche harm   er þei han hem mihte.
Þenne com on wiþ a tale   and Tholomer he telles,   525
and seis him hou Seraphe   has his men serued.
His broþer and a batayle   weore bosket bisydes,
and he sende him word   he scholde þider seche.
And þei come swiftly vppon   and swengeden togedere.
Seraphe was of hem wel war   and faste hem ascries.   530

He mette a gome on an hors   with a gret route.
He hente vp his hachet   and huttes him euene,
al tohurles þe helm   and þe hed vnder.
Wiþ þe deþ in his hals   dounward he duppes -
and þat deruede hem muche   on þat oþer syde,   535
for þe kyng Tholomer   was treweli his broþer.
Þen Seraphe fondes in,   he and fourti knihtes,
þer þe batayle was stiffest   and of more strengþe.
Þenne þei fullen for grame   to Seraphe knihtes:
þei han laft him alyue   but unneþe seuene.   540
Sikerli þe seuene   weore slayen at þe laste,
him wondet þerwiþ   and wemmet so sore
þat he was in swounynge   and fel to þe grounde.
Sone þenne he starte vp   and strei3te to his hache,
culles on mennes hedes   þat þei doun lyen,   545
siþen cacches his hors   and awei wendes.
Bote euermore Seraphe   askes and cries
where was Eualac,   þe stour was so þikke:
wel a fyue þousend men   of Tholomeres halue
weore bytwene hem two   þat to him he ne mihte.   550
And he nedde bote fourti men   folewynde his brydel,
and þei were weri of fou3ten,   and feor ouercharged
of þe peple afurst   and þe pres after -
luyte wonder hit was   so þey wrou3t haden.
Þenne was Eualac taken   and woundet ful sore,   555
and þe kyng Tholomer   takes him to kepe,
ferde into a forest   faste bisyde
forte fallen him feye   er þei a3eyn ferden.

Þenne he vnkeueres his scheld   and on þe cros
biholdes.
He sei3 a child strau3t þeron   stremynge on blode,   560
and he bisou3te him of grace   as he was godes foorme.
Þenne he sei3 a whit kniht   comynge him a3eines,
boþe armure and hors   al as þe lilye,
a red cros on his scheld   seemed him feire -
rydes to Tholomer   rad wiþ þat ilke,   565
baar him doun of his hors   and harmed him more,
strok him stark ded   þat he sturede neuere.
Siþen he fonges forþ   a ferly wepne,
fel hem fei3e to his feet   þat him hedde folewed;
þenne he horses Eualac   on Tholomeres steede,   570
bouwes touward þe batayle   bigly and swiþe.
Euermore Eualac   askes and cries
where was Seraphe,   and sei3 him wiþ þat ilke
wher seue knihtes him han   sikerliche asayled
and titli bigonnen   to take him bi þe bridel.   575

Þe white kniht wiþ his swerd   swyngede to hem sone.
Whon þe sixe weoren dede   þe seueþe a knyf cauhte,
and wolde ha striken Seraphe   at a stude derne
vppon an hole of his helm,   and he was so forfouȝten
þat he hedde no space   spedly himseluen   580
for to do him no dispit: þe sporn was his owne.
Whon Eualac þat sauȝ   he fel to þe grounde,
and Seraphe also -   and boþe lye [on] swoune.
Þe white kniht lihtes doun   and boþe hem vp liftes.
Þer nas no lynde so liht   as þise two leodes   585
whon þei blencheden aboue   and eiþer seiȝ oþer.
Þenne seis Seraphe: 'Scheuȝ me myn hache,
and I schal note hit today -   my strengþe is so
                                                newed.'
'Haue her on,' seis þe white kniht,   'vppon my
                                                bihalue.
God sende þe þis   þat al þe grace lenes.'   590
Whon he hedde hit in honde,   he heold hit þe betere
and þe heuior bi fer   þen he biforen hedde.
Nas þer ȝong mon ne old   þat ȝernloker wrouȝte
þen Eualac and Seraphe   whersoeuer þei souȝten,
also fresch as þe hauk,   freschore þat tyme   595
þen þei foundeden þidere   in heore furste come.
But euermore þe white kniht   hem þe place roumede.
Hit falles not for to seiȝe   þe fere of his duntes:
þer he lousede his hond   he leyde hem on ronkes,
and welde hem biforen   at his oune wille.   600
Þe stiward of Tholomer   stoffes hem togedere
and seis þei ben amiddes þe reume   and mowe not hom
                                                reche,
ne heo knowe not in þe lond   forþi þei moten lenge.
Þenne þe folk of þe roche   hem in face kepten,
maden þer a siker werk   and slowen hem vp clene.   605
Eualac and Seraphe   wonder hem þhouȝte
wher þe white kniht bicom   þat won hem þe prys:
þei nuste where he was   ne on whuche syde.
Þenne seis Seraphe   þat hom he wolde wende
(he is woundet ful sore)   to winnen his ese.   610
'Trewely,' seis Eualac,   'þow schalt wiþ me to court,
and two wonderful men   þou schalt seo þere.
Þei tolde me of vche a poynt   ar I fro home wente,
al togedere of þis werk   hou hit is wonne.'

Nou we leuen þe kyng   and of Ioseph carpen,   615
þat restes him in Sarras   bileued wiþ þe qweene.
'Hou trouwestou of my lord?' heo seis.   'Tydes him
                                                hele?

```
Has he fol fulsened þe sawes    þat þou bifore seidest?'
'3e, þorw þe miht of God    þe maystrie is wonnen,
and þorw his swete grace    þe sarrest is passed.'           620
'3e, I wol bihote þe heer    þi lawe for to holden.
Whon þat my lord is comen,    þat schal I furst fongen.'
'Do me sikernesse þerto,'    seis Ioseph þenne.
'I wole my trouþe þe bitake    I wol þe nout trayse.'
'Nay, þou hast non,' seis he,    'for certeyn soþe.          625
3e han be fastned wiþ hem    þat ferden wiþ luitel.'
'Tel me what is þin,    and what hit signefyes.'
And he tolde hire anon    trewely himseluen.
And heo rikenede a3eyn    radly and sone
also redili as he,    and wonder he hedde.                   630
'I schal sei3e þe, Ioseph,    for certeyn soþe,
hou I tok Cristendom    and in what tyme.
While my moder lyuede    heo hedde an vuel longe,
and sou3te into diuerse studes    and mihte haue non
                                                      hele.
Þenne wonede an hermite    faste bisyde:                     635
semely vppon a day    þidere we sou3ten.
Heo bad þis hermyte    he scholde hire hele sende.
"I am sinful as þou," he seis.    "I mai þe non
                                              graunte."
"No mak þi preyere to him," heo seis,    "þat þin hope
                                                is inne?"
"Woldestou leeue vppon him," he seis,    "I wolde þe         640
                                                    bihote
þat þou scholdest ben hol    ar þou henne eodest."
He made hire to knele adoun    and a bok bradde,
radde a gospel þeron    and bad hire vp rise.
And heo was lihtned of hire euel    in a luytel stounde.
Þenne heo seide to me:    "Dou3ter ful deore,                645
woltou beo as I am    and on þis man leue?"
And I wepte water warm    and wette my wonges,
and seide his bert was so hor    I bad not on him leeue.
And he seide to me:    "Dou3ter, he is feirore
þat þi moder has ihelet    nou in þis tyme                   650
þen I or þou    or out þat is formed."
And I tolde him a3eyn    and he so feir weore
as my broþer is at home,    I wolde on him leeue.
"Sikerly, dou3ter," he seis,    "so may grace sende
þat þou mi3t seo him þiself    ar þow henne seche."          655
Þenne com Ihesu Crist    so cler in himseluen,
aftur þe furste blusch    we ne mi3te him biholden,
ant a wynt and a sauor    whappede vs vmbe.
We weore so wel of vrself    we nuste what we duden.
He vsede of Goddes bord    and a writ brouhte,               660
```

bitauȝte me and my moder   murily to holden.
Þus Cristendom I tok   in þat ilke tyme.'
'Whi hastou let so longe   þi lord þis lyf leden?'
'Sire, forsoþe,' heo seis,   'syker I ne dorste.
He is so feol in himself   for noþing beknowe [I]   665
bote herkene of God   whon he his grace sende.
Hastou not herd þiself   hou euel he was torne?'

Now þe kyng comes to Sarras   and mony on him suwen.
As sone as he com hom,   I hete þe forsoþe,
he askede after anon   nomeliche þeose tweyne,   670
sette him on his bed   and hem on eiþer syde.
'A, Ioseph,' seiþ þe kyng,   'soþe aren þi wordes
þat þou toldest me furst.   ȝor foundeour be blesset!'
'Ho is þat?' seis Seraphe,   and [he] onswerde sone:
'He þat halp þe wiþ sound   fro þe seue knihtes,'   675
tolde hem vche a poynt   þat þei wrouȝt haden.
Hou he wuste þerof   wonder hem þouȝte.
Þenne com on fro þe fiht   þat foule was wemmed:
was striken of þat on arm   and bar hit in þat oþer.
Þen Ioseph asked þe kynges scheld   and bad þat mon   680
                                        knele:
þe arm helede aȝeyn   hol to þe stompe.
Þenne com Seraphe   and fullouȝt furst askes.
In þe nome of þe fader   Ioseph him fulwede,
and calles him Naciens   and his nome tornde.
He was þe forme þat day   þat fongede trouþe.   685
Whon he baptised was   þis oþere biheolden:
heom þouȝte he leomede as liht   al on a lowe;
þei seȝen þe holy gost   at his mouþ descenden,
and he speek þenne   þat biforen ne kneuȝ.
Þenne com he wiþ þe sore arm   þat þorw þe grace was   690
                                        holpen.
In þe nome of þe fader   Ioseph him folwed,
clepe[s] him Cleomadas   and calle[s] him after.
Þenne com þe kyng Eualac   and fullouht askes.
In þe nome of þe fader   Ioseph him folwede,
called him Mordreyns,   'a lat mon in trouþe.'   695
Þen com þe folk   to Iosaphe so þikke
he tok a basin of gold   in boþe two his hondes;
vppon þe heiȝe Trinite   he let water hiȝe
and hedde fulwed bi non   mo þen fyue þousend.

Þenn seis Iosaphe   þat Ioseph his fader   700
mot abyden him   and dwelle þer stille,
while þat he and Naciens gon   nouþer þei nusten
forte cristene þe folk   and casten þe false.

But þere an vnsely kyng   in prison hem caste
wiþ muche serwe to himself   siker atte laste,   705
for þe kyng Mordreyns   com with such strengþe
forte liuere hem out: on lyue he lafte none.
Siþen þei bitauȝten þe blod   twei burnes to holden,
and þei lenden of þe toun   and leuen hit þere.

NOTES ON THE TEXT

Abbreviations:
H   = *Estoire del Saint Graal*, ed. Eugène Hucher:
      numbers following H are page references)
MED = *Middle English Dictionary*
OED = *Oxford English Dictionary*

1   The original beginning of *Joseph* is lost with folio 402 of Vernon; see Introduction, p.viii for a discussion of how much may have been lost. The extant copy opens after Joseph's release from a captivity of 42 years, which Joseph believes to have lasted only three days, from Friday to Sunday (the specific mention of Sunday is specific to H): 'Et Vaspasiens li dist: "Joseph combien quidies-vous avoir demouret en ceste prison?" Et Joseph dist: "Sire, jou i quide avoir demouret des vendredi jusques a hui et jou quit qu'il soit hui diemences ..."' (H 115). Even given a-verses as brief as 65, 109, it is improbable that the full a-verse has been retained. Skeat (p.53) plausibly imagined 'the first extant line to form a part of some such sentence as this -
      "I passed to þis put   and to prisoun eode
      On Frydaye, sire," he seis   "and sonenday is
                                               nouwe."'

7   The English author omits an episode in which Joseph successfully pleads with Vespasian, Jerusalem's conqueror, for the life of Caiaphas, who is cast adrift in an open boat. The English version then re-arranges the order of the source, postponing the *vois* of 21 until after Joseph's baptism (at the hands, in the source, of St. Philip) and the conversion of Vespasian and his followers.

12-20   Skeat's note on this passage requires modification: 'This piece is not in the French; nor is it clear whence it is derived' (p.53). In fact, lines 13 and, in one detail, 18-20 are a loose summary of the source in its longer version, which records that Vespasian's baptism was not revealed until his second, punitive, expedition to destroy the city 'devant cou que il vinrent entre lui et son pere, destruire Jherusalem de la grant destrussion qui fu anscois que crestientes fust en la terre Agrippe le fil Herode' (*H* 122). Vespasian's father (12) is supposedly Titus, Emperor of Rome. Vespasian is the *he* of 17 and the subject of *made* (14). The plural pronouns in the passage, to the end of 17, refer to Jews living in Jerusalem. The details of the revenge visited on these by Titus and Vespasian are not derived from the French, which says 'de cou ne parole-on plus' (*H* 123). In its bloodthirsty humor the passage is reminiscent of the alliterative *Siege of Jerusalem* and other English works such as *Titus and Vespasian*, but the detail has no strong parallel in any English work. Vespasian turned the Jews out of hiding (13) and caused them to jump, or be thrown, down a drop of fifty feet (14). Skeat proposed that they fell into the pit 'where they had formerly imprisoned Joseph' (p.54), but this goes far beyond the sense of the passage. The passage's relative lack of specificity, and gruesome sarcasm (15, 17a) - together with the casual plucking of Herod Agrippa's name from the source - suggest a freehand improvisation by the English author on the theme of Jerusalem's destruction, loosely based on a recollection of the *Bible en Français*. Compare the *Middle English Prose Translation of Roger d'Argenteuil's Bible en Français*, ed. Phyllis Moe, Middle English Texts 6 (Heidelberg, 1977): the ditches of Jerusalem were filled with human carrion (p.84); when Vespasian entered Jerusalem all hidden Jews were sought out and destroyed - here by burning (p.88); and as a result of Vespasian's manoeuvers 'many fill doun into the dichis of the cite for sorow and for dispeire' (p.85).

21-5 *a vois*: Christ, who instructs Joseph and his family, with whatever followers they can convert, to leave Jerusalem forever to travel as roaming evangelists with no provisions but the Grail. They are never to return to Jerusalem once they have left (25).

30-2 Joseph has obeyed Christ's commandment and taken no provisions, relying on divine grace. His followers become worried (30a). There are some grounds for emending 30b to *summe [ben] behynde*, but I have refrained from this since the verb 'to be' can be understood from context. The phrase means that they straggle or lag behind (*MED behinde* adv., 3, 4) -

because they are disheartened. The English deftly, if flatly, epitomizes a long passage in the French (*H* 123-4), from which the English author derives his verb *demayȝen* (31): 'Et Joseph lou respondit: "... ne vous esmaies vous mie"'(*H* 123).

36   *Argos*: *H* (124) 'agais', which the source explains as a derivation from the verb 'agaiter', to ambush. The English ignores the etymology, though the corruption of the name may be scribal.

37   *Damas*: Damascus.

38   The speech is given to the second person of the Trinity, as the source implies: '"Joseph, iou sui tes Diex, tes sauverres ..."' (*H* 126).

39   *whucche*: 'ars' (*H* 127), 'huche' (Sommer, p.20).

40   þat *ilke blod*: typically, the English translator alludes to the Grail's contents rather than its container. See also 52, 297, 708. Further, 'the English author omits the request for daily prayer before the ark [*H* 127], since at no time does he treat the vessel either as an object of supplication or source of provisions' (Lagorio, "*Joseph of Arimathie*", p.94).

43   *touche*: 3p.sg.pr. subjunctive: 'and let no man touch me except you and your son.' The source is better preserved in Sommer, p.21: 'Mais iou ne voeil mie que nus touche a lescuele fors tu & tes fils.'

52a   The English author's interests in the suitability of alliteration for expressing energetic movement, skilfully deployed in the battle passages below, is demonstrated here less happily in his translation of 'A tant s'empart Josep' (*H* 127).

55-6   Unless the English translator was working from an exceptionally corrupt copy of his source, these lines are an excellent demonstration of his casual skimming, verging at times on inattention. For the source (*H* 128, Sommer p.21) notes at some length that Saracens are named after Sarras, rather than (as some mistakenly think) after Sarah, Abraham's wife.

63-4   Evalac 'wished to take counsel from his people and march against (the enemy) again; but they have refused, and he sits there, angry and distressed.'

67-8   'If you would listen to me, I should promise you that he who is my creator, who died on the cross and redeemed me so dearly, can remedy it.'

71b: *of scute red*, 'of scant judgment.' From the Vernon reading, *of scutered*, Skeat constructed a past participle, of which 'there seems to be no other instance' (p.86) and for which he gave the meaning 'frightened out of one's wits.' Neither form nor proposed meaning is at all plausible. The simple rearrangement proposed here gives a variant on the meaning of the a-verse. For *scute*, OED cites the entry from *Promptorium Parvulorum* giving as Latin equivalents *curtus* and *brevis*.

71-4   A long exchange in the French (*H* 132-5) is drastically reduced to its theological bone and given colloquial sinew.

72b   *what may he don þerate?*: 'what can he do about it?' or 'what can he have to do with anything?'

75-100 This section of Joseph's speech is translated closely, and accurately, with relatively little condensation of the French (*H* 135-8 and Sommer, pp.22-3: the shorter version here runs strikingly parallel to the English).

82   *b[e]*: Vernon *bi*, which is not (see Glossary) a scribal variant for *be* and must therefore be an error.

83   *He*: 'she'. The change of expression has been transferred by the English author, more dramatically, from before the announcement of the impending birth: 'Qant la pucele oi la parole, si en fu moult esbahie' (*H* 136).

83b-84a '"Biax sire, coument porra chou avenir, ja ne connui-jou onques nul houme carnelment"' (*H* 137).

88   *gretnede*: 'grew great' with child. This is the only recorded instance in *MED* (*gretnen*, v.), but it is a

89a   Where the source speaks again of the Holy Spirit's descent, the English author uses an auxiliary, *wolde*, which minimizes Trinitarian complications and emphasizes Christ's divine choice in the manner and time of his nativity: cf. 241b, *hou he cros souȝte*.

95a   *foure þousend and seue score*. Some versions of the source put the number at 144,000, and this seems to be what *H* (138) intends by 'VII vins et IIII mille', i.e. (7 x 20 + 4),000. The English author misunderstands the grammar of his source's arithmetic.

99-104   The detail of falling temples in 100 follows in sequence from the French (*H* 138), but the English author uses the opportunity to omit his source's brief account of the crucifixion and resurrection by returning, neatly and logically, to what was actually in the French an earlier speech of Joseph's: '"il te converra tout premierement destruire et depechier les ymages que tu aoures ... eles n'ont nul pooir de te aidier ..."' (*H* 133).

105-10   The English writer then returns to the end of Joseph's long speech on the nativity, and continues to translate closely and faithfully. Again, the resemblance to the shorter version of the French (Sommer, p.24), in which this exchange is limited to one speech by Evalac and Joseph respectively, is stronger than that to the longer version (*H* 140-1), in which there are two speeches on each side. This is not necessarily evidence against Barron's argument that the translator used the longer version, since the habitual compression of the English translation may accidentally mirror a comparable process in the shorter French version; but it emphasizes Barron's caution against a definitive statement. See Introduction, p.xxx.

111-16:   This is a paraphrase of a moderately long speech in the source (*H* 141-2), but it does not justify Skeat's note that 'this speech is given at great length in the French romance' (p.56). Skeat appears to have confused this speech with the one beginning at 121.

117-20   See Introduction, p.xxx.

121-36   This is a drastic summary of the French (*H* 143-51),
         and so extreme is the compression that it is not
         always clear. One can hardly escape a sense that
         the translator felt unhappy in face of the wordy glee
         with which his source expounds Trinitarian complexit-
         ies. 121-3, for example, lack alliteration and
         present difficulties of comprehension; it is possible
         that the translator sketched them in as a rough draft
         and intended to revise them subsequently, or even
         that the Vernon editor decided on abridgment of a
         fuller English translation. However, the salient
         points of Joseph's French speech are included; what
         is omitted is the pulpit rhetoric.

121-2   The sense is as difficult as the ellipsis is extra-
         ordinary: 'He (God) was his (Christ's) father, and
         called (father) for his (Christ's) sake, who (God)
         was regarded (as Christ's father) in spirit before
         he (Christ) was made man.'

124b   *as I beforen seide*. The line-filler, independent of
         the French, is unfortunate, since as the Vernon copy
         stands the Holy Spirit has merited only a brief
         mention in 81. This may be a further reason for
         postulating some editorial dislocation in Vernon, but
         there are other explanations less flattering to the
         English redactor. One might sympathize with Evalac's
         incomprehension.

125-6   'Although he (the second person) descended low (to
         earth), he did not forfeit his godhead so as to
         cease to be God ever after, with his great power.'
         145-6 have the same meaning.

131-2   [a]*redde*: Vernon *dredde*. I can make no sense of the
         Vernon reading as it stands and propose emendation to
         aredde, 'redeem', taking it to be an infinitive and
         most to be 3p.sg.pt., not an adverb: 'The nature of
         the mother which he adopted on earth perished,
         because he had to redeem it.' 132b would then stand
         as a shorthand summary of the reasons for Christ's
         incarnation grandly enunciated in the source (*H* 147).
         The emendation is restricted to one graph, and it is
         quite easy to confuse Anglicana lobed a and looped d
         - especially, if the hypothesis is correct, in
         circumstances where the scribe may understandably
         have lost track of the meaning.

141a   *bote I pertly vndo*: 'unless I promptly explain.'

152b   *bar him in herte*: MED records this instance under *beren*, v, sense 6e (reflexive), 'keep in mind, be mindful of', and the reading is supported by *H* (152): 'et si pensoit dedens son cuer que il fust de haute gent.' The king 'looked at Joseph's face, then at his legs, and saw he was barefoot. It struck him that Joseph would have been of noble blood (i.e., looked the gentleman he really was) if only he had been suitably dressed.' In the source Joseph has already introduced himself by the time that Evalac feels pity; the English author's delay, and small-scale amplification of his source, makes for greater drama. Evalac is moved despite himself by the saint, not by the doctrine.

169   The introduction of Josephes in the English is abrupt; in the French (*H* 153-4), Josephes has a long speech which marks him out for Evalac's attention. Its omission here is perhaps a sign of the English redactor's desire to concentrate on Joseph, the father.

171a   Again, this is closer to the shorter version: '& il li demanda sil sauoit de letres' (Sommer, p.27) - typically, rendered here into direct speech.

173   *lette lede*: this is an unusually scrupulous elision of the French (*H* 155), where Evalac calls his sergeant to take Joseph and his company 'a un moult riche ostel.'

175   The transition, like that of 212, is a direct translation of the French (*H* 155).

177   'Et moult estoit entrepris de deux pensers' (*H* 155). The detail is omitted in the shorter version, but the English author seems to have added one (181) to the number of Evalac's concerns. Barron, however (pp. 188-9), points out that other manuscripts of the longer redaction contain a passage omitted in *H* alluding to the virgin birth.

179b   þat, i.e. Joseph; *he*, i.e. Evalac.

181   [*treos*]: I adopt an emendation proposed by Skeat but

not incorporated into the text of his edition. Some noun is called for, and *treos* (cf. 191b) is sufficiently close in form to þ*reo* to account for the scribal omission. The source is clearer: there is only one tree with three stems or trunks (*H* 156).

185-6 'That (the stem with the dimmer bark) signified Jesus Christ. Because of our nature he was not so bright on the outside - but inside he was pure.'

187-90 Evalac calls his chamberlain, who comes from bed only to fall in fear; Evalac picks him up and gives the soothing advice of 189b and 190. The swoon occurs in the French after 208; the English repeats it in 203.

189 Skeat suggested that '*feres* ... may be an error for *beres*, which is alliterated to *bad*' (p.57); but the argument from meter is not strong enough to justify emendation, and I follow *MED* in recording a highly unusual sense of *ferien*, v. The episode is a much condensed rendering of the French, with emphasis placed more on the dramatic reactions of the witnesses than on the vision itself.

195 See Barron, p.190, for the range of colors offered in different manuscripts of the source; *he seis* probably means 'he sees' rather than 'he says.'

196 'Our poet uses the word *wiht* (wight, person) unadvisedly; no person spoke the words, but they were written on the stems. Or we may, perhaps, take *wiht* in the more unusual sense ... viz. creature, thing, object' (Skeat, p.57). It offers some solution, perhaps, to take it that the English author has Evalac and the chamberlain alternately ('þe wiht'; 'þat wiht', 197) read the inscriptions aloud. As Skeat added, 'the allusion to the Trinity is sufficiently obvious.'

204 The King's second vision, again much abbreviated in translation, symbolizes the immaculate conception.

208 *fore sei*[ʒ]*en*: Vernon *fore seiden*. As perhaps in 195, I believe this to demonstrate some scribal difficulty in distinguishing forms of the verbs 'to see' and 'to say'. Vernon's reading is glossed by

MED, *foresaien*, v, as 'explained (beforehand)', which makes no sense whatever here. The translation is too brief to derive conclusive support for my emendation, which means 'saw before (them)', but there are several references to the act of seeing and none to speaking. Indeed, 'li roys et ses cambrelens qui estoit avoec lui, fu si esbahis et si peureus que il n'osoit mot dire de la bouche' (*H* 161).

211   *wende*: Skeat (p.92) suggests a scribal error for 'wonde' (cf. 180); but the Vernon reading, which is clear, is supported by *H* (161): 'entra.'

212   See 175, n.

215-16a   'Unless I convert him now, before he leaves, he will never be converted'; 'car il se pense que se il n'est ore mis el point de croire, il n'i sera jamais mis' (*H* 162): again, direct for indirect speech.

225-6a   'You promised Holy Church to increase her power in order to exalt your godhead'; a precarious rendering of the French: 'Glorieus sires Diex, or est-il drois que tu rendes a sainte eglyze chou que tu li as promuis. Car tu le dois essauchier et acroistre par tout le monde' (*H* 166).

230-2   The longer version provides a heavenly voice (*H* 166-7), but this speaks much in praise of Josephes and does not instruct Joseph *père* to beget Galahad that night; still less does it give license for the lugubrious speed with which the command is fulfilled (232). The subsequent narratorial comment, on the chaste relationship between Joseph and his wife, gives rise to an anecdote demonstrating that 'it was only by direct command of God that their son Galahad was born' (Barron, p.185). There follows the brief praise of Galahad which montions Britain (*H* 168). Lagorio, "*Joseph of Arimathie*," p.95, does not show any familiarity with Barron's work but comments interestingly on the 'author's confused or disinterested conflation of Joseph's second son with the future Grail knight.' There is no need for any more sophisticated explanation; the author's respect for his source at this point is scarcely more than a random collection of stray phrases from every third or fourth sentence. There is, however, a conscious cross-reference to the *Queste* (see Introduction, p. xxvii); but there is little else to indicate Arthurian interest on the part of this author. The interference with the source's divine voice also helps to upstage Josephes *fils*.

234 *reises*: Skeat's transcription, 'roises,' is an error. The subject is Joseph.

235 þester may be a verb, in which case it is an archaism; or it may be an adjective, as in 160, with 'to be' understood (cf. 30, n). The storm is transposed, since it occurs in the source after morning prayers in front of the ark. The alteration may be meant to detract from the Grail: it is Joseph's and his son's prayers which move Christ, not their location before the ark. Yet it achieves the opposite, implying that the storm is the penalty for their lateness with matins before Joseph's *whucche*.

240-56 This crucial speech is much condensed (*H* 170-4), but clear in structure, sense, and salient points.

244 *bote*: 'but (afterwards).'

245 *Bote*: 'unless.'

247 *bote*: 'only.'

247-8 'They (the prophets) had only the Holy Spirit - and you have that too, and then as well you have me in the flesh (to be) at your will' (i.e. in the eucharist).

251 *Iosaphe*: Josephes *fils*, whose role in the *Estoire* was determined by Joseph's non-celibacy; see Introduction, p.xxiii.

256 *but elles*: 'except.'

257b Ellipsis in Vernon of the subject pronoun, *he* meaning Josephes.

258-312 This represents a major reshaping and abbreviation of the source, which proceeds in the following order: (i) Josephes' vision of the crucified Christ within the ark; (ii) Josephes is called to communion by

Christ himself, seated on a rich throne (the Siege Perilous), and consecrated bishop with the same oil with which all the kings of Britain were anointed up to the time of Uther Pendragon; (iii) a long exegesis of the virtues symbolized by Josephes' episcopal vestments; (iv) Christ's injunction giving Josephes spiritual guardianship of the people, and his father corporeal guardianship; (v) the eucharist, with a long and sensual description of transubstantiation; (vi) God's assurance that Evalac will be converted (*H* 174-96). The English author translates (i) quite fully (258-98), being, as usual, studiously vague about the Grail (297b); (ii) is ruthlessly summarized in 299-300, and all Arthurian references are deleted; (iii) becomes one line, 301, which lacks alliteration and looks like an unrevised first draft; (iv) is translated crisply in 306-10; (v) is omitted and (vi) is represented by 311. The temper of the English redaction is readily identifiable. While strongly interested in the marvellous, (i), and retaining what of (ii) and (iv) is essential to an understanding of the son's (and father's) apostolic mission, the somewhat mannered religiosity of the source is suppressed. There is indeed a slightly spurious quality to the pious dilation of the French account of investiture and Mass; the affective piety is being used to sanctify the Grail, and therefore the Arthurian quest, at one remove.

261b *of queynte hewe*: 'toute uermeile comme sanc' (Sommer, p.32).

274-5 The syntax is highly paratactic, and the variation on two forms of one verb *renne/eornen* is infelicitous: 'Josephes looked at his feet, saw (blood - and water?) running from them, streaming with red blood flowing everywhere.' The author is trying to represent the sheer number of references to blood at this point in his source; but these lines again have an unrevised appearance.

276 This is a line of summary inserted by the English translator to catch up the thread of the narrative, and also, being *aa/ax*, his form.

277 Again the English effectively substitutes direct speech for the French's indirect.

281-4   There is a change in the order of the source here to
        make the climactic view of the risen Christ (*H* 179)
        coincide with Joseph's joining his son at the ark
        (*H* 177). 282 and 283 lack binding alliteration across
        the verses, and clumsily repeat *seȝen*; again there is
        an improvised, or disjointed, quality.

288   *wasscheles*: 'vessels': 'orcueil' (Sommer, p.34);
        'orcuel' (*H* 178).

291   'Apres, en vit issir un autre qui avoit letres en
        son front escriptes, et si disoient: "Jou sui
        apieles force del tres haust segnour."' (*H* 178-9).
        The English author helpfully solves the riddle:
        Gabriel ihoten.

292   þe *riccheste sege*: the Siege Perilous, but here not
        identified.

295-8   This detail (*H* 177) would have followed 281 had the
        translator kept to the order of the source. There
        follows a large hiatus in the translation, for one
        misplaced detail of which see 313-23, n.

300   *boto*: see Glossary - an archaism.

301   This one line, without convincing alliteration
        ('*v*estimens'/'signe*f*yen'?), stands in place of six
        pages of Hucher's edition (*H* 185-91).

304   *anoyg*[*n*]*ten*: Vernon *anoygten*, with probable
        omission of a contraction sign.

313-23 The drastic rearrangement of 258-312 is followed by
        a truly wayward decision on the translator's part.
        313, 319, 320 and 322 lack any binding alliteration,
        and the alliteration is also defective elsewhere:
        these are by now familiar signs of haste. For the
        sprinkling of holy water around the palace, the
        English text returns to the end of the vision of
        Christ crucified, where the action is performed not
        by Joseph and his followers but by angels. Thus the
        source for 313-14 comes from *H* (180): 'A tant passa
        toute la compagnie par devant iaus; si alerent
        envirounant tout le palais dedens, et par tout la u
        il aloient gietoient li angle l'aighe au gieteour,'
        and the source for 315 is Christ's explanation of

the act: 'Naitoiemens des lieus u li mauvais esperis
a converseit; car ceste maisons a este tousjors
habitacles au diable' (*H* 180). The alteration is so
great, and so without point, that one is forced to
wonder whether the English translator quite understood
his source, or whether some scribal error has bungled
the original order of his work.

For the inscription on the wall of the palace,
317-23, the English backtracks even further to *H*
168-9: 'Ichil lius u il estoient herbergie et il
ouroient, si estoit uns palais, qui estoit apieles
li palais esperiteus. Et cestui non li avoit mis
Danoiaus le prophete, qant il repairoit de la bataille
Nabugordenosor le roi, qui l'avoit pris entre les
autres juis, qant il l'enmena en Babiloine. En cel
repaire, passa Daniaus par cele citet, et qant il
vint el palais, si vit escrit en la porte letres de
carbon en ebriu, et disoient que cil palais ert
esperiteus. Chil nons fu acoustumes a dire si
c'onques ne kai et tant com li palais sera en estant
sera-il apieles esperitues.' The English author's
insertion of the name *Auntres*, 320, and the concrete
interpretation of 'esperiteus' as *meruellouse for
werkes*, 324, is another sign of his determined and
unpretentious conversion of spiritual mysteries into
showcase miracles. Again, however, the backtracking
is inaccurate, pointless, and uncharacteristic of a
redaction which elsewhere demonstrates an exemplary
ruthlessness.

317   *wordes*: 'letres' (see above, 313-23, n). Skeat's
'werdes' is a mistranscription.

324   The English now returns to *H* 197 from which it
deviated in 313. The sole function of the messenger
in the French is to get Joseph and his company to
Evalac's palace; since, as a result of the tinkering
in 313-23, they are already there, one might judge
his introduction wholly redundant.

327   '... si se drecha uns clers qui qui [*sic*] estoit
tenus au plus sage et au plus fonde de lour loy' (*H*
198). A variant version such as Sommer's, 'al miex
fonde' (p.42) may have influenced the b-verse.

337-42   This is a close but reduced translation of the French,
and manages to give its gist quite crisply: 'Car se

>li peres et li fix et li sains esperis n'avoient que une seule deytet, donques n'estoit mie cascuns d'aus trois, entiers Dius ne parfais, dont ni prendront noient la piersonne del fil ne del saint esperit; et s'eles avoient ambesdeus la deyte enterine, dont seroient-chou trois deytes, ne chou ne porroit nus contredire raisnablement. Car nus hom qui chou contredist, ne porroit raisnablement prouver ne metre en voir que l'une des trois personnes eust entiere deyte en lui, u nule des autres fust amenteue.' (*H* 198).

339-40   *igraunte*: Skeat reads 'I graunte,' which makes less sense. I take the lines to mean: 'If each one has a godhead conceded to him separately, then each one is as much a true god as the three together' - i.e. they are three, not one.

343-6   The English author is notably kinder to Joseph than his source: 'Qant chil eut si durement parle encontre le deytet et encontre le trinitet, si fu Joseph moult esbahis del desfendre et del prouver encontre ce que chil avoit dit. Si ne seut mie maintenant respondre a fausser cou que chil avoit dit. Car a nostre seigneur ne plaisoit. Lors se drecha Josephes maintenant, et si parla en haut si que de tous fu derenement ois et dist au roy ...' (*H* 199).

349   *iseȝe*: 'seen'; *toniht*, i.e. 'last night.'

350   The meaning is not entirely clear: 'You have disclosed matters about which God is not pleased,' i.e. Evalac's failure to believe in the Trinity and immaculate conception. This is a line of summary rather than direct translation, and it lacks binding alliteration. The speech as a whole is condensed.

353   *Tholomer*: probably the son of the benefactor of Evalac (below, 425); þat þou weore wont to hunte: 'Et chil qui tousjours a este fuitis, encacera celui qui tousjours l'a cachie' (*H* 200). The translation is too specific.

359   In the source, Josephes has already threatened the clerk with summary retribution should he persist in arguing.

370   *lym[p]e*:   Vernon 'lyme.'

371   *to fonge þe trouþe*: 'to adopt the true religion.'
        The line is a very brief summary of Josephes' answer
        in the French, and lacks any alliteration.

372   *þis mon*, i.e. the clerk, who is now blind and dumb;
        tides him hele?, 'will he recover?' The question is
        never answered; it is rather a stage-device to shift
        the scene to the temple.

379   *þat [me] clepeþ Martis*: Vernon reads ȝe, but the
        scribe was probably confused by *me*, 'men', and
        rationalized what he took to be a pronoun. For *me*
        with singular verb, see Karl Brunner, *An Outline of
        Middle English Grammar*, translated by G.K.W. Johnston
        (Oxford, 1970), p.68. The source reads 'Martirs que
        il clamoient le dieu de la bataille' (*H* 205).

382   In the source (*H* 205-6), it is the devil in the idol
        of Mars who in his agony destroys the images of Mars
        and Apollo. The English author seizes the opportunity
        to improve Joseph's saintly credentials.

385   The line is an improvised, and ineffective,
        transition: does *him* refer to the clerk of 372, or
        to the devil clinging comically to the ceiling?

387   *his pors*: this may refer to Evalac's own purse but
        is more probably that placed before the idol. The
        English has softened Evalac's idolatry: 'si vaut
        sacrefier; mais Iosephe ne li laissa, ains li dist
        (tel sacrefice) quel il se faisoit tel sacrifice,
        que il morroit de mort subite' (*H* 206). 390 is
        therefore a highly literal translation.

389-90 'If you offer him anything I guarantee that I shall
        cause you to die suddenly'. I take *to preue* to be an
        adverbial phrase, glossing *preue* as a noun (*OED*
        'proof', sb., sense 5): compare *Destruction of Troy*
        5525: 'Epistaphus, to preue, was his pure nome.'

390   See 387, n. The English repeats the pleonasm of the
        French.

399-402 'Et Josephe sailli avant, et se li dist: "Je te
        conjur par la force de la sainte trinitet que tu en

dies le voir." Et li diables respondi que il ne li savoit riens dire de chou qui li estoit a avenir' (*H* 207). As well as transposing the idol's reply into direct speech, 402, the English amplifies the source in 399b: the result is a line without alliteration.

403a   Cf. 324a: the formula is varied in the source.

405   *Nagister*: French readings of the name are variably 'Onage,' 'Onagre' (*H* 208).

406b   The present tense has a future sense: Evalac will manage to relieve the siege.

407   *Alongines*: 'Elavachin' (*H* 208); 'ualacin' (Sommer, p.46).

410   The perfect has a future perfect sense: see 406, n.

414   *bounen*: *MED* follows Morris (Skeat, p.61) in judging this, the scribal reading, 'make ready, arm,' an easy error for *bonnen*, 'assemble or summon.' This is possible, but reference to the French does not resolve the question. In the shorter version we read: 'Maintenant fist li rois *semonre* tout son pooir & les fist *assambler* a carabel' (Sommer, p.46); but the longer version has a phrase which would completely justify *bounen* as an unusual alliterative verb (cf. *Scottish Field*, 113): 'Maintenant fist li roys semonre tout son pooir, et manda ... que il fuissent au sesime jour *tout appareillet d'armes* a Tarrabiel' (*H* 208-9). Since the Vernon scribe is unusually definite about minim graphs, and since the source evidence is inconclusive, I have let the harder reading stand.

416   *Carboye*: 'Tarrabiel' (*H* 209); 'carabel' (Sommer, p.46). The distance the castle stands from Sarras and from 'Alongines' differs, as do many such details, among various manuscripts of the source, and there is little agreement with the English redaction.

419   *Ioseph*: the source gives this long speech to 'Josephe,' i.e. *fils*, but the alteration in the English is conceivably deliberate.

423   i.e. Evalac's father was a cobbler.

425   The story in the source is that Augustus Caesar, disturbed by reports of Christ's imminent birth, demanded tribute from all countries subject to Rome. Evalac was sent as page to two daughters of Count Sevain, lord of Meaux, who were a portion of the agreed tribute. On their death he was sent by Tiberius to the Count of Syria, whose son he later killed after a quarrel. He escaped to Babylon and helped old king Tholomes conquer Holofernes, whose kingdom he received as thanks.

436   The English adds the detail of Tholomer's extreme age in an attempt to distinguish between him and the Tholomer presently attacking Evalac. The French is vague here, and the distinction is made necessary in the English by the freehand rendering of 353.

438-9   *For ... forþi*: 'because ... therefore.'

440   *co*[*nne*]: Vernon *come*n. The line stands in place of a short penitential sermon in the French (*H* 212-13), and its sense is inept without emendation. I suspect a minim misreading, perhaps as a result of contractions, by the Vernon scribe, and translate: 'It's not at all (the time), sir king, to speak about what we (i.e. the Christians) know.' This introduces 441, and makes Joseph's polite refusal to continue to act the oracle, 443-4, a repetition of 440. Typically, the English makes Joseph more practical in his concern: Evalac has a war to fight. In the French, Josephes replies: 'tu ne le sauras devant la que tu aies depechies les ymagenes que tu aoures ...' (*H* 213).

441   [*hede*]: Vernon omits a necessary noun.

445   For Evalac's white shield with its red cross, see Introduction, *The Source*. British enthusiasts finally appropriated for St. George the device borrowed by the French authors from the Templars. The source attributes the donation to Josephes, not Joseph.

454   *þei tornede aȝein*: 'Evalac's men retreated.' Meanwhile, however, his subjects in 'Alongines' have sacked Tholomer's camp.

456-7	This episode is a drastic summary, without alliteration in 457. The author generally throughout the battle sequence ignores or condenses the more precise tactics of his source, and pieces together episodes to convey an appropriately martial atmosphere.
458	The detail has no license from the source and is thoroughly inappropriate: Evalac is supposed to be downhearted and overwhelmed, in no mood for a lakeside half-holiday. The line may well be a mistranslation of a detail in the longer version only, that the messenger rides to meet Evalac 'sour un grant rouchin courant' (*H* 223) - that is, on a large running horse. The English translator, it seems, has taken 'rouchin' to be cognate with forms such as 'ruissel,' a brook or stream.
461	This is a more fortunate addition to the French.
468	*þe two Cristene men*: the source (*H* 223) mentions Josephes only.
469b	*I trowe hit be þeraboute*: 'I think it must be about this.'
471b	This is an addition to the source and anticipates Evalac's first prayer to Christ in battle. It is barely conceivable that the verse marks a return to direct speech as the herald reports on prayer at court, but the assumption is unnecessary. The English makes Evalac more sympathetic than the French, which itself frequently hints that his heart is growing progressively receptive to Christian truth even though his actions lag behind - as his baptismal name will imply (695, n).
472-4	This is a change to the structure of the source, inserted from later in the battle sequence: 472 merely repeats 414, and 473 lacks alliteration. In the English version, Evalac's men answer his summons as if by overnight express; the French is more realistic in 414 (see 414, n, 'au sesime jour') but not here (*H* 226).
490	Cf. 451: this seems to be a favorite collocation.

491	Ellipsis of subject 'þei': 'that they who followed his advice should not, through him, regret their course of action.'
493	þenkes ou, 'think, remember,' reflexive; not, as Skeat transcribes it, 'þenkes on.'
494	and: 'if.'
495-6	Having omitted the tactical details before battle, the English author produces two affective lines for Seraphe's peroration in his highest alliterative style. The heroic sentiments are based on Evalac's speech in the source: 'jou ne sai que jou die (plus); mais nous devons bien savoir tout que est hounours et que est hontes. Si gardons que nous ne fachons tel cose pour paour de mort u de prison dont nous soions hounist a tousjours mais; ne que il soit reprouvet a nos enfans apries nos mors.' (*H* 234)
507	Þere were stedes to str[iu]en 'there were places to fight in.' Vernon reads struien, and Skeat accepted this reading: 'there were horses to be destroyed.' The passage is a fairly free rendering of its source, but there seems to be an equivalent section in the French: 'Et qant les lanches furent pechoies et li coutel et li faussart et les grans haches trenchans d'achier furent traites, si fu illuec si grans li capleil, et la meslee fu si mortex, que des espees que des haches et d'autres fieremens dont il feroient sour les hanches, et sous les hiaumes, et sour les escus et sour les haubiers, que chou estoit avis que chou estoit une grande merveille de forgeours' (*H* 236-7). The opening emphasis falls on the 'capleil,' slaughter, and 'la meslee,' although there are later details of cavalry warfare which justify 511 and 517. But 507 is the beginning of the battle sequence, and an introductory a-verse equivalent in meaning to the b-verse is perhaps to be expected. On str[iu]en/struien: although the Vernon scribe is unusually careful with minim graphs, he may easily have been misled by a less careful original, and would in any case have read 'struien' if he understood stedes to mean 'horses.' The evidence from alliterative collocations is ambivalent, showing both a stour: striue collocation ('Wondir stalwart and strang to striue in ane stour,'

Golagros and Gawain, 353; 'Full stithe was þe stoure for þe striffe new,' *Destruction of Troy*, 6787) and a *stede* (= horse): *stour* collocation ('Mony stithe man in stoure on stedis enarmyt,' *Destruction of Troy*, 1179; 'Thay stekede stedys in stoure with stelene wapynes,' *Morte Arthure*, 1488); *Destruction of Troy* 28 ('of the stoure and þe stryffe when it distroyet was') joins both *striue* and *struien* with *stour*. The principle of *durior lectio* is inapplicable. On balance I am persuaded that the conjectural emendation proposed here makes for a more logical (and, in view of 511 and 517, less repetitive) opening to the combat, which corresponds more closely to the French and is at least plausible palaeographically.

522 *a roche*: 'In the French, Tholomer's men flee, and are pursued by Seraphe and Evalac to a narrow pass, where there was a rock which was named afterwards the "Rock of Blood" from the great loss of life there in this battle. Evalac left some men there to keep the pass, and a second skirmish afterwards took place there' (Skeat, pp.63-4). The Rock is introduced late in the English, and the sign of structural dislocation - no alliteration in 521-2, no binding alliteration in 523 - is present.

527 Tholomer's brother is called 'Manatur' in *H* (246): he has been sent by Tholomer to fight Seraphe, and is killed in 536.

539-40 This summary account of the source lacks binding alliteration.

546 In the source Seraphe seizes the horse of a knight whom he has killed, and there may be a slight hiatus in the Vernon copy between 545 and 546. Alternatively, the English redactor may have been happy to change the details, in which case *his hors* refers to Seraphe's own horse.

552 *weri of fouȝten*: 'exhausted with fighting,' a traditional collocation with the past participle as gerund. Cf. *Partonope of Blois*, ed. A.T. Bödtker, EETS OS 109 (1912), line 11142, and see R.M. Smith, "Three Notes on the *Knight's Tale*," *MLN* 51 (1936), 320-22.

555   This last line of drastic summary lacks alliteration.

558   The English is more bloodthirsty than the French, which says only that Tholomer wished to disarm Evalac and his knights, who were still in their armor (*H* 254).

560   *child*: Christ; see *MED* child, n, sense 2b.

562   'Then he saw a white knight riding to meet him.' The white knight is an angel.

563   'et si eut a son col un escut blanc a une vermeille crois et ses chevaus estoit autressi blanc qu'une flours' (*H* 255).

564b   *seemed him feire*: either 'seemed to him (Evalac) beautiful,' or, more probably, 'suited him (the angel) well.' The French has only 'a une vermeille crois' (*H* 255; 563, n).

565   *rad wiþ þat ilke*: 'immediately.' This is a drastic condensation of the French.

567   In the source the white knight does not kill Tholomer but takes him prisoner (*H* 257); news of Tholomer's death reaches Evalac and Seraphe after their return to Sarras.

572-3   Cf. 547-8: the sudden affection between Evalac and Seraphe, whom Evalac formerly mistreated, is meant to illustrate the growth of *caritas*.

583   [*on*] *swoune*: Vernon *swoune*; cf. Skeat, '[a] swoune.'

585   The simile, like that of 595, is not from the source. It is also proverbial (B.J. Whiting, *Proverbs, Sentences and Proverbial Phrases from English Writings mainly before 1500*, Cambridge, Mass., 1968, p.330), but there is only one recorded example, from the highly alliterated Harley Lyrics, before *Piers Plowman* B, I 156 (ed. George Kane and E.T. Donaldson, London, 1975): 'Was neuere leef vpon lynde lighter þerafter.' Given the context - the growth of Christian love, exemplified in the friendship of Evalac and Seraphe - this is a plausible source for the image in *Joseph*.

592   þe heuior bi fer: this appears to be a mistranslation,
        for the French reads 'plus legiere' (*H* 259). Perhaps
        the English author is thinking of its effect on the
        enemy.

598   fere. The choice is between MED ferd, n., 3, power
        (as Skeat took it) and MED fere, n., 5, manner. I
        prefer the latter: the white knight's strength has
        already been established, and the English author is
        excusing himself from further narrative detail.

601-03 'Tholomer's steward, named Narbus, rallies his men,
        and they attempt to retreat by the pass of the "Rock
        of Blood"; but "the folk of the Rock" (i.e. those
        left by Evalac to guard it) utterly rout them'
        (Skeat, p.65). The speech beginning at 602 is not
        appropriate in the mouth of Tholomer's steward, and
        the þei of 602 and heo of 603 must refer to
        Tholomer's folk. Has a line been lost between 601
        and 602? The corresponding passage is *H* 262-3.

606-07 These two lines are summary rather than translation;
        the author seems to have conceived of their
        alliteration across the two b-verses. The English
        has moved to a later section of the source (*H* 285).

611-14 This is close translation: 'Et li roys respondi que
        il voloit que il s'envenist a Sarras, car il li
        mousterroit les plus grans merveilles que nus hom ne
        peust quider ne croire d'un houme qui li avoit dit,
        a son mouvoir, toutes les coses qui li estoient
        avenues en la bataille' (*H* 286). Even so, 611-13
        lack alliteration. However, a drastic structural
        alteration occurs immediately after 614.

615   The transition is again a direct translation from
        the source (*H* 264), to which the English backtracks
        to tell the story of Queen Sarrasinte. Joseph in
        the English takes over the role of his son from the
        source.

621-44 Sarrasinte's tale begins with faithful translation,
        condensed after 630 (*H* 265-9).

627   þin: i.e.'þin trouþe', your faith, supplying the
        noun from 624. In the French (*H* 266), Josephes
        speaks, and the Queen flawlessly repeats 'tous les

poins de la foi et de la Trinite.' Skeat's proposal that both simply repeat 'the creed' (p.65) seems entirely in tune with the less ambitious English redaction.

640 *woldestou*: 'if only you would ...'

642 The English redactor characteristically omits the teaching by which Sarrasinte's mother is converted by the hermit Salustes. The redaction of this episode becomes more abbreviated from this point.

645 *heo*: Sarrasinte's mother.

645-8 Sarrasinte 'thinks her mother refers to the hermit, and replies that she will not believe on one so old and gray, but only on one who is as fair as her own brother' (Skeat, p.65). 648 neatly translates the source: 'jou li dis pour chou que il avoit trop grant barbe' (*H* 270).

652 *he*, i.e. Christ.

661 'he gave the writing to my mother and me to keep joyfully.' The *writ* of this line does service for the hermit's teaching of the Christian religion, which the English omits, and for: 'Ensi nous ensegna la loy Jhesu-Crist a tenir' (*H* 272). The English version then omits a long stretch of the source (*H* 272-83) which details further miracles concerning the deaths of Sarrasinte's brother, her mother and the hermit.

665 *beknowe [I]*: Vernon reads *be knowen* (with a line ending after *be*). I can make no sense of the reading as it stands, whether regarding *beknowen* as two words or one (= *MED biknouen*, sense 2). Emendation is necessary, and the most plausible - taking *beknowen* to be one word - rests on the assumption that the scribe mistook a capital I in his original for a contraction mark followed by a paragraph sign or virgule (this argument has particular force if the scribe's copy text was also written in prose format). Lines 665-6 then translate: 'He is such a cruel man in himself that on no account do I confess anything, but wait for God to send his grace.' This makes some sense as a shorthand rendering of the French: 'jou

	atendoie tant que Jhesu-Crist, par sa pitie, m'envoiast le point convegnable de lui metre a raison, mais jou n'en fui onques encor en point, car me sires est uns hom moult crueus ...' (*H* 283). For my translation of *for noþing*, cf. 219b, *for noskunus þinge*.
671	*his bed*: it is Seraphe (*H* 287) who is resting 'en une couche.'
674	[*he*]: Vernon omits a subject. The speaker is Joseph.
676	This is a highly condensed summary of the source and lacks alliteration.
679	'uns hom ... [qui avoit tantost le pong encope] ... portant son poing seniestre tout copet en la diestre main' (*H* 289-90); see Barron, p.192, and for the equivalent detail in the *Queste* see Introduction, p.xxv.
686-9	The baptism of Naciens follows the source closely (*H* 292); the fire of 687 is the form of the Holy Spirit in 688.
687a	Proverbial: see Whiting (585, n), p.339.
692	*clepe*[*s*], *calle*[*s*]: Vernon reads *clepen*, *callen*, but the subject is still apparently Joseph (cf. 683-4). I have preferred present to past inflexions on the grounds that the scribal confusion is more likely to have arisen in the present tense. *Cleomadas*: 'cou fu autretant a dire comme Gonfanonniers [standard-bearer] au glorieus seigneur' (*H* 293).
695b	The name Mordreyns is explained in the French as meaning 'tardif en creance' (Sommer, p.75) and this verse is a literal translation of the phrase. The English version surprisingly omits a potentially amusing exchange in the French, when Evalac discovers that his wife has been a Christian for 25 years.
696-9	With an eye to 700, the English redactor reluctantly reintroduces Josephes *fils*.

697-8	'Et Josephe tenoit un grant bachin d'argent, si viersoit a cascun sour la tieste, el non de la sainte Trinitet' (*H* 294).
699	*mo þen fyue þousend*: 'cinq milliers et trois cents et cinquante-neuf' (*H* 294); as usual, however, the number varies greatly in different manuscripts of the source.
704	There is a possibility of scribal omission of two or three lines of text here (see Introduction, p.xxix). The English redaction of the *Estoire* is interrupted by a compressed translation of a passage from the *Queste*: see Introduction, p.xxvii.
708-09	See *H* (295), where Josephes names three men, not two, to guard the ark.

GLOSSARY

(The aim of this glossary is to present all material necessary for translation of the text and judgment on its language. In the alphabetical presentation þ follows *t* and *ȝ* follows *y*; vocalic *v* precedes consonantal *v*.)

abak, adv., back, away, 496; 'abac', 453.
abascht, pp. (*MED abaishen*, v.), perplexed, upset, 202.
Abrahames, Abraham's, 56.
abrod, adv., widely, so as to cover a wide space, 501.
abyden, v., remain, (reflexive), *or* wait for (trans.), 701; 'abyde', wait for, meet, 357.
adoun, adv., down, 642.
adred, adj., afraid, 47.
aferd, adj., afraid, 203, 412.
aftur, prep., after, 88; 'after' 266; adv., 321, 446.
afurst, adv., (*MED afurst*, adv. (1)), first, first of all, 553.
agrisen, v., shudder with fear, 3p.pl.pr., 236.
allynge, adv., in any way, at all, 440.
Alongines, the name of a castle, 407.
also, conj., as, 113, 340, 595, 630.
amende, v., to mend, repair, 423.
amiddes, adv., in the middle, 445; prep., 602.
amorwe, adv., in the morning, 34.
and, conj., if, 48, 73, 389, 494; elsewhere = and.
an heiȝ, see *heiȝ*.
anon, adv., immediately, at once, 188, 452, 467, 628, 670.
anoþur, adj. & n., a second, 179; another, 378.
anoyg[n]ten, v. (*MED enointen*, v.), to anoint, 304.
apertliche, adv., distinctly, 276.
Apollin, Apollo, 376; 'Appolin', 380, 383.
ar, conj., before, 122, 127, 215, 655. See *er*.
arayes, v., sets in order, 3p.sg.pr., 451, 490.
[a]redde, v., (*MED aredden*, v., sense 2), to deliver, save, redeem, 132.
Argos, the name of a forest, 36.
Aramathie, Arimathea, 156.
armure, n., armour, 563.
ascries, v., (*MED ascrien*, v. (1), sense 2(b)), challenges and attacks, 3p.sg.pr., 530.
asemblet, pp., engaged in combat, 520.
asur, n., blue, 195.
at enes, see *enes*, adv.

atte, prep. + definite article, at the, 281, 356, 705.
atwo, adv., to pieces, 103.
atwynne, adv., apart; *louse a.*, open, 49 (*MED atwin*, adv., sense 1(a)).
auenturus, n., adventures, destiny, 232.
Augrippus, (Herod) Agrippa's, 19.
Augustes Cesar, 75, 424.
Auntres, adj. (*MED aventurous*, adj., sense 4), marvellous, 320.
auter, n., altar, 295.
auȝte, see *ouȝte*.
ay, adv., then, at once, 98; 'ay forþ', ever after, 126.
aȝein, prep., towards, to meet, 'aȝeynes', 459, 562; against, contrary to, 106.
aȝein, adv., back (again), 12, 25, 207, 629, 681; in reply, 652; in return (*MED ayen*, adv., sense 7), 393.

Babiloyne, Babylon, 318, 354.
bad, see *bidden*, v.
bale, n., death, destruction, 502.
bar, see *beren*, v.,
baronage, n., nobility, 62.
batayle, n. (*MED batail*, n.), battalion, body of warriors, 527 (sense 3); battle, 318, 571 (sense 2a); fighting, 538 (sense 1).
bed(en), see *bidden*, v., and *biden*, v.
behynde, adv., with verb 'to be' understood: lag behind, straggle, be at a disadvantage, 30.
beknowe, v., confess, reveal, 1p.sg.pr., 665.
ben, v., to be, 87, 89, 189, 248; 'beo', 323, 388, 646; 'b[e]', 82 (see note); 1p.sg.pr., 'am', 646; 2p.sg.pr. (with fut. sense), 'beost', 308; 3p.sg.pr., (with fut. sense), 'beos', 216; 3p.sg.pr.subj., 'beo', 169, 388; 'be', 469; 2p.pl.pr., 'ben', 66; 3p.pl.pr., 'beon', 168; 'ben', 140; 'beþ', 409, 'beoþ', 331; 'aren', 672; 2p.sg.pt., 'were', 428, 435, 'weore', 428, 430; 3p.sg. pt.subj., 'weore', 447; 'were', 122, 652; 3p.pl.pt., 'weore', 20, 25, 33; 'weren', 317; sg.imper., 'beo þou', 47, 80; pl.imper., 'beo ȝe', 245; pp., 'iben', 153; 'ibeo', 469; 'be', 626; 'ben', 153.
bente, n., battlefield, 450, 489.
beo, prep., by, 366. See *bi*.
beotake, see *bitake*
beotime, adv., promptly, 465.
beren, v., to bear, carry; 2p.sg.pr., 'berest', 40; 3p.sg.pr., 'beres', 261, 262; 'bereþ', 396; 3p.sg.pt., 'bar', 286, 679; 'beer', 502; 3p.pl.pt., 'beeren', 453; carry (a child), 82; 'baar him doun of his hors',

           unhorsed him, 566; 152, 'bar him in herte', *MED* gives
           sense 6e (reflexive), kept in mind, was mindful of -
           see note.
bernes, see *burnes*.
bert, n., beard, 648.
Betanye, Bethany, 29.
bi, prep., by, 42, 136, etc.; 'beo', 366; concerning, 169
           (*MED bi*, prep., sense 9a); *bi þat*, at that time, then,
           324 (*MED* sense 4e).
bicom, v., *either* had come from *or* had gone (to), 3p.sg.pt.,
           607.
bidden, v., beg, 3p.sg.pt., 'bad', 637; ask, 3p.sg.pt.,
           'bad', 442; 3p.sg.pr., 'biddes', 461a; offer,
           'beode', 387; urge, advise, 3p.sg.pt., 'bad', 31,
           84, 189; 3p.sg.pr., 'biddes', 461b; command, 3p.sg.
           pr., 'biddes', 22, 26; 2p.sg.pt., 'bad', 219;
           3p.sg.pt., 'bad', 233, 257, 268, 643, 680; deliver
           (a blow), 3p.sg.pt., 'bed', 502; wish, intend,
           1p.sg.pl., 'bad', 648.
biden, v., stay, remain, wait, 3p.sg.pr., 'byden', 450;
           pp., 'beden', 416; wait for, 3p.pl.pr., 'bydes', 468.
bifalle, v., happen, 488.
biforen, adv., in front, 28, 600; before, previously, 85,
           118, 592, 689; 'bifore', 618; (mentioned) before,
           271; 'beforen', 124, 'bifore', 143, 'byfore', 270;
           as a preliminary, 'bifore', 406.
biforen, prep., into the presence of, 167; in front of, 362.
biggore, adj., stronger, 452.
bigly, adv., vigorously, 571 (mainly alliterative poetry).
bihalue, n., 'vppon mi bihalue', at my request, on my
           authority, 589.
biheete, see *bihote*.
biheolde, v., watch, 3p.pl.pt., 'beheolden', 686; 3p.sg.pr.,
           'biholdes', 260; look, 3p.sg.pt., 'biheold', 151;
           3p.sg.pr., 'biholdes', 274, 559; look at,
           'biholden', 657.
bihote, v., to promise, 621, 640; assure, 'biheete', 67.
bileeue, n., belief, doctrine, 358.
bileued, pp. as adj., left behind, remaining, 616.
bineoþe, adv., underneath, 192.
bireuen, v., to take away: 'þi lyf bireuen', 356, put you
           to death (*MED bireven*, v., sense 3b).
bisyde, adv., nearby, 54, 522, 557, 635; 'besyde', 457;
           'bisydes', 527.
bitake, v., entrust, 253; 1p.sg.pr., 'beotake', 306; give,
           pledge, 624.

bitauȝte, (biteche, v.), gave, 3p.sg.pt., 'bitauȝte', 661; entrusted, 3p.pl.pt., 'bitauȝten', 708.
bi þat, (1) adv., at that time, then, 324; (*MED bi*, prep, sense 4e).
(2) conj., by the time that, 473 (*MED bi*, conj., sense 1).
biþenke, v., refl., reflect, consider, 3p.sg.pr., 'biþenkes him', 237 (*MED bithinken*, v., sense 1).
blenchen, v., 'blencheden aboue', looked up, 3p.pl.pt., 586.
blusch, n., look, glimpse, glance, 657 (*MED blish*, n., sense 2, first recorded instance).
blyue, adv., promptly, without delay, 7.
bodiliche, adv., corporeally, in the flesh, 248, 309.
bone, n., prayer, 227 (*MED bon*, n(2), sense 1(b)); command, 268 (*MED bon*, n(1), sense 3).
bord, n., table: 'Goddes bord', altar, communion table, 660; boards, 'bordes', 204.
boren, pp., born, 168, 430.
boske, v., see *buske*.
bote, (1) prep., except for, 43, 97; 'bote elles', 256;
(2) conj., but, 57, 133, 186 etc.; unless, 141, 245; except, 130;
(3) adv., only, 338; 'nedden bote', had only, 247, 551.
boto, num., both (*MED bo*, num., sense 2, archaic); for 'boto his hondes', 300, see also *MED bothe*, num., sense 2a(g).
boþem, n., bottom (of pit), 15.
boun, adj., prepared, ready, 26, 461.
bounen, v., make ready, arm, 414, 'boune', 472.
bouwe, v., to go; pres. part. 'bouwynde', 294; 3p.pl.pr., 'bouwe', 489; 3p.sg.pr., 'bouwes', 571 (*MED bouen*, v(1) sense 6: alliterative sense only); 387, 'bowes', 3p.sg.pr., is either the above *or MED* sense 4a, to lean over.
bracen, v., enshrouded, wrapped, 'ibraced', pp., 265; 'braset', pp., tightly held, 380.
braset, see *bracen*.
breken, v., smash, 103; 3p.sg.pt., 'breek', 501; 3p.sg.pt., 'brak', broke (intransitive), 384.
bren, v., burn, 103.
brimme, n., bank, 458.
broþer, n., brother, 478, 653.
brouȝtest, brouhten, see *grounde, honde*.
brusede (brisen, v.), injured, 3p.sg.pt., 501.
Brutayne, Britain, 232.
burþe, n., birth, 93.

burnes, n., humans, people, 708; 'buirnes', 29; soldiers, 501, 'bernes', 414.
buske, v., prepare, get ready, 3p.sg.pr., boskes, 414, 472; pp., bosket, 527 (*MED busken*, v., sense 1(b)); arrayed, 3p.sg.pt., 'bosked', 111; pp., 'ibosket',153 (*MED* sense 3(a)); to go (hastily), march, hasten, 3p.sg.pr., 'buskes', 202, 233, 354, 450 (*MED* sense 4); 3p.pl.pt., 'bosked hem', 13, the same but reflexive (*MED* sense 4(c)).
byden, see *biden*.

cacches, v., catches, snatches, grabs, 3p.sg.pr., 546; 3p.sg.pt., 'cauȝte', 365; 'cauhte', 577.
calle[s], v., 3p.sg.pr., names, 692.
Carboye, the name of a castle, 416.
carke, v., be anxious about, concerned about getting, 3p.pl.pr., 30.
carpe, v., to speak, 440; 1p.pl.pr., 'carpen', 175, 212, 615.
casten, v., defeat, refute, 703; contradict yourself, 2p.sg.pr., 'castest þiseluen', 117; threw, 3p.sg.pt., 'caste', 704.
cauȝte, see *cacches*.
chaumberleyn, n., chamberlain, valet, 187, 203.
chaumbre-wouh, n., chamber-wall, 204.
cher, n., mood, expression, 83.
child, n., i.e. Christ, 560, 206 (*MED child*, sense 2); 'childre', children, 493.
clanses, v., cleanses, purifies, 3p.sg.pr., 198.
clene, adj., excellent, 408; pure, 186, 251; adv., completely, 250; altogether, 406.
Cleomadas, the knight whose arm was healed, 692.
clepen, v., call, 3p.sg.pr., 'clepeþ', 379 (see note); 3p.sg.pr., 'clepe[s]', 692.
cler, adj., bright, attractive, 186.
clergye, n., learning, 171.
cloþes, n., (altar) cloths, 295.
come, n., approach, advent, 206; arrival, 596.
coma, v., come, 25; 3p.sg.pt., 'com', 9, 21, 99, etc.; sg.imper., 'cum', 251.
con, v., have ability, knowledge; 1p.sg.pr., 402; 1p.sg.pr. subj., 'cunne', 48; 2p.sg.pr., 'const', 401, 421; 3p.sg.pr., 'con', 171, 214; know, 1p.pl.pr., 'co[nne]', 440.
coroune, n., crown, 263.
counseil, n., council (meeting), 62; (secret or confidential) consultation, 469; advice, 471.
cristene, v., baptise, convert, 703.

crois, n., cross, 293, 446; 'cros', 241, 261, 326.
cuiþe, v., demonstrate, do, 484 (*MED kithen*, v.).
culle, v., strike; 'culles on', beats upon, 3p.sg.pr., 545
    (*MED killen*, v.).
cumpanye, n., company, 27.
cun, n., kin, 422.
cunne, see *con*.
cuntre, n., country, 37.
cuþþhe, n., country, 18; 'kuþþe', 434.

Damas, Damascus, 37.
Daniel, 221, 318.
dedeyn, n., 'haven dedeyn', take offense, be scornful, 244.
defaute, n., fault, responsibility, 307.
demayȝen, v., to be alarmed, 31; 'demayen', 84.
deore, adv., dearly, 69.
dere, adj., fine, excellent, 37; 'deore', dear, 645.
derne, adj., secret, insidious, 578.
derue, v., harm, 47; 3p.sg.pt., 'deruede', 535 (rare).
digne, adj., worthy, 252 (with 'to' = of).
discounfitede, pp., defeated, routed, 61.
diskeueret, pp., disclosed, divulged, 350 (see note).
dispit, n., injury, 581.
diȝen, v., die, 495; 'dye', 390; 3p.sg.pt., 'diȝede', 132, 134.
diȝt, pp., as adj., ready, prepared, 34; 'idiht', armed, 476.
dimmore, adj., dimmer, 183.
don, v., do, 26, 72; 3p.sg.pr., 'dos', 233; 1p.pl.pt.,
    'duden', 659; 3p.sg.pt., 'dude', 90; pp., 'do', 524; cause,
    'do', 389; 3p.sg.pr., 'dos', 252; 3p.sg.pt., 'dude', 129;
    sg.imper., 'do', 311; put, 'do', 40; sg.imper., 'do', 102;
    give, sg.imper., 'do', 623; 'don hem to ȝonge', set out, 34;
    'haue to done', be busy, have (things) to do, 161 (*MED don*,
    v., sense 9b); 'do tel me', please tell me, 391 (auxiliary
    for pleading or emphasis; *MED* sense 11a).
dorste, v., dare, 3p.sg.pt., 357; 1p.sg.pt., 664.
douhtilyche, adv., valiantly, 495.
douȝter, n., daughter, 645, 649; pl., 'douȝtres', 426.
douȝti, adj., noble, 480 (*MED doughti*, adj., sense 2).
duntes, n., strokes, blows, 598.
duppes, v., falls (*MED dippen*, v., sense 3(b): distinctive
    use), 3p.sg.pr., 534.

Ebreu, Hebrew, 317.
eft, adv., then, again, 268, 359.
Egipte, Egypt, 60, 98.
eir, n., heir, 19.
eiþer, num., each (of them), 286, 586, adj., 671.

eiȝen, n., eyes, 362.
elles, adv., in another way, 119; 'but elles', except for, 256.
enes, adv., once, 25; 'at enes', at once, 51, 181, 517.
eni, n., any one, 307.
enkes, n., colours, 194.
eodest, see *gon*.
eornen, v., run, ?3p.pl.pr., 275: see *renne*.
eorþe, n., the earth, 131, 254; ground, 100.
er, adv., formerly, at first, 243.
erest, adv., originally, 56.
Eualac, King of Sarras, 365, 520, 548, etc.; 'Eualak', 214, 518; 'Euelak', 347.
euel, n., disease, 644; 'vuel', 633; evil, 190.
euel, adj., difficult, 667.
euene, adv., straight, 57, 113, 532.

face, see *kepen*.
fader, n., father, 12, 118, 121, etc.; genitive sg., 'fadres', 249.
falle, v., fall, 3p.sg.pt., 'felde', 203; 'fel', 582; 3p.pl.pr., 'fallen', 362; 3p.pl.pt., 'fellen', 516; happen, turn out to be, 190; engaged with, 3p.pl.pt., 'fullen', 539 (*MED* senses 25, 28); 'hit falles not', it is not necessary, 598 (*MED fallen*, v., sense 39): see *felle*.
faren, v., go, 506; 3p.sg.pt., 'ferde', 28, 557; 3p.pl.pt., 'ferden', 54, 368; 'fare to hem', advance on them, attack them, 63; 'aȝeyn ferden', returned, 558; 'ferden wiþ', experienced, practised, got along with, 626 (*MED faren*, sense 8); 'ferede trewe', came true, 413.
faste, (1) adv., close, 54, 457, 522, 557, 635; closely, hard, 530; tightly, 380;
  (2) adj., fast, secured, 272.
fastenen, v., put (blame on), charge, 249; pp., 'fastned', associated with, 626.
faus, n., (*MED fals*, n., sense 2): 'wiþouten faus', for a certainty, truly, 208.
faute, n., blemish, 208.
fayn, adv., eagerly, 179.
faynede, v., fawned on, flattered, 3p.pl.pt., 243 (*MED fainen*, v., sense 4, unusual).
feble, adj., weak, 65 (see *semblaunt*).
fei, see *feyþ*.
feire, adv., fairly, well, 243, 564.
feirore, adj., fairer, more beautiful, 649.
felauschupe, n., sexual intercourse, 84; company, 165.

felde, see *falle*.
felle, v., (confused in forms with *falle*), strike, knock down, 368; 'fallen', 558; 3p.sg.pt., 'fel', 569.
fend, n., devil, 385.
feol, adj., evil, formidable, fierce, 222, 665 (*MED fel*, adj.).
feole, adj., many, 18, 90, 100, 147, 238.
feor, adv., greatly, 552; 'bi fer', by far, 592.
feorþe, adj., fourth, 264.
ferd, n., fear, 188; 'fert', 18.
ferd, adj., afraid, 189.
ferde, n., company, 12.
ferde(n), see *fare*.
fere, n., manner, 598 (see note).
feres, v., 3p.sg.pr., lifts, 189 (*MED ferien*, v., sense 3: only recorded example).
ferli, adv., wonderfully, 154.
ferli, n., wonder, astonishment, (at), 210.
ferly, adj., terrifying, marvellous, 568.
fert, see *ferd*.
fette, v., fetch, bring, 3p.sg.pt., 12, 147; 'lette fette', had brought, caused to be brought, 167; brought, pp., 'ifet', 428.
feye, adj., dead, mortally wounded, 368, 558; 'feiʒe', 569.
feyþ, n., faith, 11; 'fei', 245.
fle, v., fly, 3p.sg.pt., 'fleyʒ', 385; 3p.pl.pt., 'flowen', 362; take flight, 3p.sg.pt., 'fleih', 98; 3p.pl.pt., 'flowen', 18.
fleschliche, adv., fleshly, in the flesh, 135.
flescly, adj., carnal, 107.
flote, n., company, 28.
floures, n., flowers, 35.
flowen, see *fle*.
fluiʒt, n., flight, 506.
fol, adv., fully, 618; 'ful', very, 645.
folfulle, v., remedy, 68.
folwed, folewede, folewen, see *fulwe*.
fond, v., found, 3p.sg.pt., 242, 462; 3p.pl.pr., 'founden', 33.
fonde, v., test, 3p.sg.pt., 'fondede', 505.
fondes, fondet, see *founde*.
fondede, see *fonde*.
fonge, v., accept, subscribe to, 371; 'fongen', 622; carry away, 3p.sg.pr., 'fonges', 52; 3p.sg.pt., 'fongede', 685 (*MED* sense 5); assumed, 3p.sg.pt., 'fongede', 143 (*MED* sense 6); grasp, draw, 3p.sg.pr., 'fonges', 568 (*MED* sense 1).

fontston, n., font, 7.
foorme, n., form, 282, 561.
foote, n., feet (of measurement), 14; 'fot', (anatomical), 52.
for, conj., because, 428, 438.
for, prep., *either* for the sake of (*MED for*, conj., sense 2) *or* in spite of (*MED* sense 9), 85; for the sake of, 399.
foretelle, v., mention (beforehand), 1p.sg.pr., 110.
forfouȝten, adj., exhausted with fighting, 579.
forlet, pp., left behind (by their own), 20.
forme, adj., first, 685.
formed, pp., made, enacted, 190, 210; created, 651.
forsaken, pp., refused, denied, 64.
forset, pp., oppressed, attacked, 487.
forsoþe, adv., in truth, 3, 86, 99, etc.
forte, conj., (for) to, 15, 40, 116, etc.
forþi, adv., therefore, 439, 465; wherefore, 603.
forþinkes, v. (impersonal), grieves: 'þat me forþinkes', I regret, I repent, 487.
forþward, adv., forward, 53.
forþwiþ, prep., in front of, 259, 267.
founde, v. (trans.), approach, 367; reach, 3p.pl.pr., 'founden', 33; (intrans.), go, come, 3p.sg.pr., 'fondes', 537; 3p.sg.pt., 'fondet', 12; advanced, 3p.pl.pt., 'foundeden', 596; take (to flight), 'founden', 506; reach, 3p.pl.pr., 'founden', 33.
founden, see *fond*.
foundeor, n., Maker, Creator, 68; 'foundeour', 673.
fouȝten, pp., as gerund, 'weri of fouȝten', weary from fighting, 552.
Fraunce, France, 426.
fresch, adj., fresh, 595; comp. as adv., 'freschore', more freshly, 595.
frusschede, v., struck, beat, 3p.sg.pt., 505.
fuir, n., fire, 260.
fullen, see *falle*.
fullouȝt, n., baptism, 682; 'fullouht', 693.
fulsened, pp., fulfilled, performed, 618 (*MED fils(t)nen*, v.).
fulwe, v., baptise, 3p.pl.pr., 'folewen', 8; 3p.sg.pt., 'folewede', 70; 'fulwede', 683; 'folwed', 691; 'folwede', 694; pp., 'ifolwed', 7; 'fulwed', 699.
furst, adv., first, 9, 682 (i.e. was the first), 139, 622, 673.
furste, adj., first, 133, 139, 596, 657.

Gabriel, the archangel, 291.
Galaad, Galahad, 231.
Galile, Galilee, 77.
gete, v., get, win (over), 23; beget, 230; reached, pp., 'geten', 523; 'geten on hem', pp., advanced on them, 497; capture, 97; pp., 'geten', 410; provided himself with, pp. (refl.), 'geten him', 327.
geyn, adj., excellent, pleasing, 299.
geynliche, adv., fittingly, 298.
gleyue, n., lance, spear, 497.
god, adj., good, 66 (see *greiþe*).
gome, n., man, warrior, 531.
gon, v., go, 24, 83; 3p.pl.pr., 'gon', 702; 'goþ', 386; pl. imper., 'gos', 373; 2p.sg.pt., 'eodest', 4, 641; 3p.pl.pt., 'eoden', 326.
gost, n., spirit, 49, 315.
gostliche, adj., spiritual, 280; adv., spiritually, 122, 135, 310.
grame, n., anger, hostility, 539.
graunte, v., grant, give, 638; consented, acquiesced, 3p.sg.pt., 'grauntede', 87; conceded, conferred, pp., 'igraunte', 339.
greiþe, n., governance, control, 66; 'greyþe', counsel, 341.
greiþe, v., dress, vest, 299.
greiþli, adj., good, noble, 88.
gretnede, v., became pregnant, 3p.sg.pt., 88 (only recorded instance).
grounde, n., 'brouhten to grounde', overcame, subdued, 453.
gultus, n., sins, 249.

ha, habben, see *haue*.
hache, n., ax, 503, 544, 587.
hakken, v., hack, chop, 3p.pl.pr., 512.
halp, see *helpe*.
hals, n., throat, 534.
halse, v., entreat, implore, 1p.sg.pr., 400.
halt, see *holden*.
halue, n., ax handle, 503.
halue, n., side, 549.
haly, adj., holy, 288, 314.
haspet, pp., fastened, 205.
hauberkes, n., coats of mail (probably plated), 509.
haue, v., have, 63, 524; 'ha', 351, 578; 'han', 524; 'habben', 255; 1p.sg.pr., 'haue', 141; 2p.sg.pr., 'hast', 350, 625; 'hastou', 663, 667; 3p.sg.pr., 'has', 405; 2p.pl.pr., 'han', 246, 247, 626; 3p.pl.pr., 'han', 60, 61, 64, 102, 338, 469; 1p.sg.pt., 'hedde',

250; 3p.sg.pt., 'hedde', 11, 270, 271, 315, 327, 344, 503, 580, 591, 592, 630, 633, 699; 'hade', 319; 3p.pl.pt., 'hedde', 178, 569; 'hedden', 244, 246; 'hadden', 474; 'haden', 676; sg.imper., 'haue' (þou), 210, 589; 3p.sg.pl.subj., 'hedde', 153; 3p.pl.pt. subj., 'hedde', 523.

hauk, n., hawk, 595.
haunsen, v., increase, 225; advance (Britain's destiny), 232; raised, pp., 'vp haunset', 515.
he, pron., he, 1, 26, 31, etc.; with one exception: she, 83. See *heo*.
hed, n., head, 263, 533; pl., 'hedes', 515, 546.
hedde, see *haue*.
[*hede*], n., attention, 441.
heiȝ, adj., noble, 153; 'heiȝe', 698; abstruse, exalted, 159; 'hiȝeste', superlative, 254; loud, 346; aloft, 'on heiȝ', 182, 'vppon heiȝ', 503; aloud, loudly, 'on heiȝ', 209, 228; 'an heiȝ', 2.
heiȝtest, see *hete*.
heiȝþe, n., height, 192.
hele, n., health, recovery from sickness, 372, 634, 637; success, 617.
helede, v., became healed, 3p.sg.pt., 681; healed, pp., 'ihelet', 650.
helpe, v., help, 369; pp., 'holpen', 690; helped, 'halp', 1p.sg.pt.subj., 484; 3p.sg.pt., 675; to be of avail, to be effective, 3p.sg.pr., 'helpes', 226 (*MED helpen*, v., sense 3).
henne, adv., hence, from here, 215, 641, 655.
hente, v., seized, 3p.sg.pt., 382; 'hente vp', picked up, took up, 532.
heo, pron., (1) she, 87, 461, 465, 617, 629, 633, 637, 639, 644, 645, 664. See *he*;
(2) they, 97, 283, 603; accusative/dative 'hem', 31, 34, 116, etc.; 'heom', 130, 367.
heold, see *holden*.
heore, their, 18, 20, 101, 150, 242, 313, 328, 373, 521, 596; 'here', 30.
heowen, v., hew, 3p.pl.pr., 511.
her, adv., here, 306; 'heer', 621.
herbarwe, n., lodging, accommodation, 30; 'herborwe', 32.
here, v., to hear, 45, 401; 'heere', 109; 1p.sg.pr., 'here', 137; 3p.sg.pt., 'herde', 31, 346; 3p.pl.pt., 'herden', 2; pp., 'herd', 667.
herkene, v., listen, pay attention, 67; wait (for), 1p.sg. pr., 666.
Heroudes, Herod, 93; Herod's, 19.

herre, adj., higher, 430.
herte, n., mind, heart, 152 (see *beren*).
hete, v., be called, named, 2p.sg.pr., 'hettestou', 155; 3p.sg.pt., 'hette', 376; pp., 'hoten', 79, 82, 231; 'ihoten', 291; promise, 2p.sg.pr., 'hiȝtest', 109; 2p.sg.pt., 'heiȝtest', 225; assure, 1p.sg.pr., 'hete', 412, 669.
hettestou, see *hete*.
hewe, n., colour, hue, 261.
heuior, adj. comparative, heavier, 592.
hire, pron., her, 223, 225.
hise, possessive pron., his, 24, 274.
hit, pron., it, 132, 160, 226, 440.
hiȝe, v., hurry, do its work, 698.
hiȝen, v., to make famous, exalt, 226 (*MED heien*, v., sense 3).
hiȝtest, see *hete*.
ho, who, 466, 674.
hol, adj., whole, 681; as adv., 641.
holden, v., hold (with hands), 3p.sg.pt., 'heold', 360, 591; 'huld', 504 (*MED holden*, v., sense 2); keep, retain, 'holde', 220; 'holden', 621, 661, 708; 3p.sg.pt., 'heold', 134 (*MED* sense 11); defend (refl.), 3p.pl.pr., 'hulden hem', 512; pl.imper., 'holdes ou', 492 (*MED* sense 16); preserve, maintain, infin., 'vp to holde', 311; go, proceed, 3p.sg. (for pl.) pt., 'heold', 113 (*MED* sense 21); situated, pp., 'iholden', 417 (*MED* sense 23); reckoned, considered, 3p.pl.pt., 'heolden', 430; pp., 'holden', 95, 254, 328 (*MED* sense 27); regarded as, pp., 'halt', 122 (*MED* sense 27(b)).
hole, adv., together, 340.
holliche, adv., wholeheartedly, 51; completely, 86, 134; in full, 456; together, 517.
holt, n., stronghold, castle, 410.
hom, n., home, 602, 609, 669.
honginge, pres.part., hanging, 205.
hond, n., hand, 261, 262, 270, etc.; pl., 'hondes', 300, 697; 'honden', 272; 'brouȝtest him to honde', got the better of him, overcame him, 438.
hor, adj., hoary, white-haired, 648.
horses, v., provides with a horse, puts on horseback, 3p.sg.pr., 570.
hoten, see *hete*.
hou, how, 120, 526, 617, etc.
houen, v., halt, 3p.pl.pr., 489; ride, 511.
hous, n., house, 57.

hudden (hem), v., refl., hid, concealed themselves, 3p.pt. pl., 13.
huirne, n., recess, niche, 378; 'huirenes', nooks, hiding places, 13.
huld, see *holden*.
huppe, v., fall, leap, 14.
hunte, v., attack, oppress, 353.
huttes, v., hits, 3p.sg.pr., 532.

I- before past participles.
icholde, for 'ich wolde', I would, 67.
ichul, for 'ich wol', I will, 253.
idiht, see *diȝt*.
Ierusalem, Jerusalem, 24.
ifet, see *fette*.
ihelet, see *helede*.
Ihesu Crist, Jesus Christ, 38, 185, 238, etc.
ilke, adj., as intensifier, 6, 40, 279, etc.; 'wiþ þat ilke', adv. phrase, with that, then, 573.
in, n., lodging, 163.
inne, v., lodge, 166; provides with lodgings, 3p.sg.pr., 'innes', 174.
Iosaphe, Josephes, son of Joseph of Arimathea, 169, 251, 299, etc.
Ioseph, Joseph of Arimathea, 5, 7, 11, etc.; 'Iosep', 44, 65, 155, etc.
ioyned, pp., 'þou beost ioyned harde', you will be allotted punishment, 308 (*MED joinen*, v. (2)).
ioynes, v., approaches, 3p.sg.pr., 407 (*MED joinen*, v., (1), sense 9(b)).
iseo, *iseȝe*, see *seo*.
islawe, pp., slain, 96.
Israel, 218, 347.
istrauȝt, pp., stretched, 269.
iswowen, pp., swooning, fainted, 203.
Iubiter, Jupiter, 366.
iugget, pp., judged, 251.
iworpe, pp., cast, thrown, 221. See *warpes*.

kenne, v., say, tell, 158; 'kennen', 187; 3p.sg.pr., 'kennes', 198; informed, pp., 'kenned', 466; instructs, 3p.sg.pr., 'kennes', 446.
kepen, v., keep: 'hem in face kepten', 3p.pl.pt., confronted them hostilely, 604.
keuere, v., cover, 3p.sg.pt., 'keuerde', 263; pp., 'keuered', 176.

keueren, v., advance, 3p.sg.pr., 'keueres vppon', 406; 3p.
    pl.pr., 'keueren on', 27.
kneuȝ, v., knew, recognized, 3p.sg.pt., 478; knew, 689.
kuynde, n., nature, 131, 133, 139, 143; 'kuyndes', 136;
    natural law, 106; 'þe kuynde', the family, 488;
    'vre kuynde', i.e. us, 185.

lacche, v., seize, arrest, 356; sustained, received,
    3p.sg.pt., 'lauȝte', 222.
ladden, see *lede*.
laft(est), see *leuen*.
lai, leiȝen see *ligge*.
lat, adj., late, slow: 'a lat mon in trouþe', a man
    reluctant to believe, 695.
lauhwhen, v., laugh, 3p.pl.pr., laugh, 2.
lauȝte, see *lacche*.
lede, v., lead, 173; 'leden', 663; 3p.sg.pr., 'ledes', 32;
    led, 3p.pl.pt., 'ladden', 16.
lees, v., lost, forfeited, 3p.sg.pt., 125.
leeue, v., believe, 105, 108, 640, 648, 653; 'leue', 646;
    'leeuen', 219; 1p.sg.pr., 'leeue', 388; 3p.pl.pt.,
    'on leeueden', 101; sg.imper., 'leeue', 99.
lemede, v., struck, 3p.sg.pt., 264 (*MED lemen*, v. (1)).
lenden, v., arrive, come, 81; 3p.sg.pr., 'aȝein lendes', go
    back, 207; 3p.pl.pr., 'lenden of', leave, depart
    from, 709.
lene, v., grants, bestows, 3p.sg.pr., 'lenes', 590; 3p.sg.
    pl., 'lente me of', granted me (a portion) of, 5.
lenge, v., remain, stay, dwell, 162, 603; 2p.sg.pr.,
    'lengest', 277; 3p.sg.pr., 'lenges', 207; 2p.sg.pt.,
    'lengedest', 429; 3p.sg.pt., 'lengede', 17; 3p.pl.
    pt., 'lengede', 16; pres.part., 'lenginde', 20; pp.,
    'lenged', 425.
lengore, adv., longer, 137.
leodes, n., people, men, 168, 585.
leomede, shone, blazed, 3p.sg.pt., 687 (*MED lemen*, v., (2)).
leoue, adj., dear, 240.
leres, v., teaches, 3p.sg.pr., 305.
lette, v., caused, 3p.sg.pt., 94, 167, 173; 'let', 698.
leue, see *leeue*.
leuen, v., leave, 1p.pl.pr., 175, 212, 615; 3p.pl.pr., 386,
    709; 3p.sg.pt., 'lafte', 707; pp., 'laft', 540; was
    left, remained, 3p.sg.pt., 'lafte', 518; dwelled,
    stayed, 2p.sg.pt., 'laftest', 435.
leyk, n., action, activity, 17.
leyser, n., leisure, 164.
lide, n., lid, 41, 257.

ligge, v., remain, 2p.sg.pr., 'liggest', 278; lay, 3p.sg. pt., 'lai', 176; 'lay', 266; were encamped, 3p.pl. pt., 'leiȝen', 418.
lihte, v. (1), set light to, burn, 3p.pl.pr., 'lihten', 191 (*MED lighten*, v. (1)).
lihte, v. (2), alight, 3p.sg.pr., 'lihtes', 584; descend, 81; 3p.sg.pt., 'lihte', 116, 145 (*MED lighten*, v. (2)); relieved, pp., 'lihtned', 644.
liked, v. (impersonal), it pleased, 3p.sg.pt., 17.
limes, n., limbs, 151.
limpe, v., happen, befall, 213; 3p.sg.pr.subj. 'lym[p]e', 370.
liueraunce, n., provision (of lodging, food), 163.
liuere, v., deliver (from prison), 707.
loken, v., look, 3p.pl.pr., 281; pres.part., 'lokynde', 278.
loueliche, adj., gracious, 239.
loueliche, adv., gladly, with joy, 281; graciously, kindly, 305.
louse, v., set free, cause to flow, 3p.sg.pr., 'louses', 273; flexed, 3p.sg.pt., 'lousede', 599; open, sg. imper., 'louse', 49.
lowe, adv., down, 173; low, 145.
lowe, n., fire: 'on a lowe', alight, afire, 687 (*MED loue*, n. (2)).
lowore, adj., lower, 151.
lufte, n., air, sky, 385.
lust, v.impersonal, it pleases, sg.pr., 41.
lustnynge, n., attention, 164.
luttulde, grew less, 3p.sg.pt., 145.
luyte, 1) adj., little, 554; 'luytel', 39, 644; few, 506; as n., 'luitel', 626.
2) adv., little, 17, 481; 'luite', 148.
lynde, n., linden or lime tree, 585.
lyue, n., life; 'on lyue', alive, 707.

mallen, v., pierce (through), 3p.pl.pr., 508.
manas, n., threat, 46, cf. 'manas and threten', threaten, make threats.
Marie, Mary, 79.
Martis, Mars, 379.
Maudeleyn, (Mary) Magdalen, 223.
maumetes, n., idols, 102, 373.
mayden, n., virgin, 85, 119, 144, etc.; 'maiden', 80; 'mayde', 88.
maystrie, n., might, 398; victory, 619.
[*me*], n., men, 379.
medlen, v., engage (in battle), 507.

meeten, v., meet, 415; 3p.pl.pr., 508.
mekelyche, adv., meekly, benignly, 223.
melen, v., speak, 2p.sg.pr., 'melest', 106; 3p.pl.pt.,
    'meleden', 130; 'melen of manas', make threatening
    talk to, 46.
mene, v., speak, 2p.pl.pr., 379; 3p.sg.pr., 'menes', 403.
mensked, pp., worshipped, glorified, 146.
merueilouse, adj., miraculous, 322 (see note on 313-23).
mette, v., dreamed, 3p.sg.pt., 442.
miht, n., strength, power, 128, 619; 'miȝt', 146; plural,
    'mihtes', 373.
miȝt, v., might, could, 3p.pl.pr., 97; 'miȝte', 201; 3p.pl.
    pr., 'mihte', 192; 3p.pl.pt., 'mouȝten', 23.
miȝtful, adj., mighty, 508.
moder, n., 131, 135, 633; 'mooder', 98.
mon, n., man, 72, 84, 116, etc.; 'man', 122; pl., 'men',
    90, 166.
Mordreyns, (formerly Eualac), 695, 706.
morwe, n., morning, 26, 234, 473.
most, adj., greatest, 447; 'moste', 375.
mot, v., must, shall, 3p.sg.pr., 701; 2p.sg.pr., 'most', 230;
    3p.pl.pr., 'mote', 166; 'moten', 603; 3p.sg.pt.,
    'most', 132.
mowe, v., may, 3p.pl.pr., 602; 'mouȝten', might, 3p.pl.pt.,
    23.
murili, adv., joyfully, 255; 'murily', 661.
myle, n., miles, 417, 418.
myne, adj., my, 44, 240.

Nabugodonosor, Nebuchadnezzar, 319.
Naciens, (formerly Seraphe), 684, 702.
Nagister, a city, 405.
nare, v. (for 'ne are'), are not, 3p.pl.pr., 338, 342.
nas, v. (for 'ne was'), was not, 3p.sg.pt., 126, 146, 593.
Nazareth, 78.
ne, conj., not, 48, etc.; nor, 593, 603, 608.
nedde, v. (for 'ne hedde'), had not, 3p.sg.pt., 118; 3p.pl.
    pt., 'nedden', 247. See *haue*.
nede, adv., of necessity, 230.
neih, adv., nigh, almost, 203.
neode, n., need; 'at neode', in extremity, 484.
neodes, v.impersonal, pr.sg., 'al þat þe neodes', all you
    need, 163.
nere, adv., never, 357.
newed, pp., regained, revived, 588.
newely, adv., immediately, 33.
nis, v., is not, 3p.sg.pr., 66, 350, 449.

niȝt, n., nights, 6 (s. for pl.); 'niht', night, 176, 442; 'niȝt', 473.
no, neg., nor, 639 (interrogative).
nome, n., name, 10, 53, 78, etc.
nomeliche, adv., especially, 670.
nomen, pp., taken, 405.
non, n., noon, 699.
noskunus, 'for noskunus þinge', not for any reason, not at at all, 219 (*MED noskinnes*, adj.).
not, v., know not, 1p.sg.pr., 467.
note, v., put to good use, 588.
nou, adv., now, 29, 217, 310, 355, 358, 615, 650; 'nouwe', 1; 'now', 520, 668.
nout, see *nouȝt*.
nouþer, adv. (*MED nowher*, adv.), (not) where; 'nouþer þei nusten', they did not know whither, 702.
nouȝt, n., nothing, 128; 'nout', 186; of no value, account, 'nouȝt', 379.
nouȝt, adv., not (at all), 115, 125; 'nout', 206, 226, 624.
nul, v. (for 'ne wol'), will not, 1p.sg.pr., 249, 335.
nuste, v. (for 'ne wuste'), 3p.sg.pl., 199; 1p.pl.pt., 659; 3p.pl.pt., 129, 608; 'nusten', 702. See *wite*.

o, adj., one (and the same), 146, 182. See also *on*.
of, prep., out of, 385; (some) of, 404; from, 255.
on, prep., with, 560; in, 101.
on, adj. as n., one, 120, 178, 183, 200, 261. See also *o*.
onswere, v., answer, 377; 3p.sg.pr., 'onsweres', 393, 467; 3p.sg.pt., 'onswerde', 674.
op, adv., up, 336, 345; 'vp', 359, 363.
or, or, 6, 51.
or, your, 65, 248, 495. See also *oure*.
oþer, conj., or, 201, 208.
oþer, adj., second, 262; 'oþur', 271, 396; other, 297, 304, 342, 679; 'oþur', 220; another, 289, 293; 'oþur', 287; opposite, 535; as noun, 255, 364, 586; 'oþur', 271; 'oþure', 234, 294, 386; 'oþere' (pl.), 489, 686.
ou, accusative/dative plural, you, 73, 460, 461; 'ow', 67, 250, 468.
ouercharged, pp., overborne, 552.
oune, adj., own, 600; 'one', 128, alone; as noun; own (people) or (possessions), 20; own (land) or alone, 495.
oure, your, plural, 245, 373, 493.
out, n., anything, 127, 171, 369, 651; 'ouȝt', 488; adv., at all, 370.
outwiþ, adv., on the outside, externally, 186.

ouþer, adj., either, 184.
ow, see ou.
ouȝte, v., possessed, 3p.sg.pt., 36, 425; 'auȝte', 434; 'euele ouȝtest', you should not have done, 486.
oygnemens, n., ointments, oil, 303.

paleys, n., palace, 314, 316; 'paleis', 320, 322.
pallede, v., struck, knocked down, 3p.sg.pt., 499.
parti, n., a part, some, 45.
payet, pp., pleased, satisfied, 350.
peine, n., pain, 112; passion, 'peyne', 276.
pertly, adv., sharply, briskly, promptly, 141.
pleye, v., refl., amuse himself, exercise, 458.
polhache, n., pole-ax, 499.
pors, n., purse (perhaps that for offerings to the idol, rather than the king's), 387.
poynt, n., incident, 613; detail, 676; 'bi þis poynt': at this juncture (before he leaves), 215.
pres, n., tumult, press, 500.
prest, adv., quickly, 459.
preue, n., proof, 389 (see note).
preue, v., prove, 110; proved, tested, 3p.sg.pt., 'preuede', 500; test, pl.imper., 'proues', 373.
prikynge, pres.part., riding, spurring, 459.
priueliche, adv., secretly, privately 276.
put, n., pit (underground) dungeon, 4, 221.
puttest, v., 2p.sg.pr., in 'fore puttest', mention, expound, 337.

queynte, adj., beautiful, unusual, 261.

rad, adv., 'rad wiþ þat ilke', forthwith, 565; 'radly', promptly, 629.
radde, v., read, 3p.sg.pt., 643.
red, n., advice, 63, 491; judgment, discrimination, reason, 71.
redeli, adv., clearly, distinctly, 630.
redi, adj., convenient, available, 444; present, ready, 42.
reise, v., raise, exalt, 231; rouse, 3p.sg.pr., 'reises', 234.
renne, v., run, flow, 274. Cf. eornen.
reowen, v., they may regret, 3p.pl.pr.subj., 491; pities, 3p.sg.pr., 'rewes', 154.
res, n., course of action, 491.
reson, n., matter, 76; sense, reason, 138.
reume, n., realm, 352.
rewes, see reowen.
riche, n., kingdom, 307.

rihtes, v., directs, drills, 3p.sg.pr., 451, 490.
rikenen, v., relate, 76; 2p.sg.pr., 'rikenest', 138;
 recited, said over (the Creed), 3p.sg.pt.,
 'rikenede', 629.
rikenyng, n., explanation, narration, 444.
riȝt, adv., right, close, 42.
roche, n., rock, 522, 604.
Rome, n., (city of) Rome, 75, 424.
romynge, pres.part., running, flowing, 275.
ronkes, n., rows, 599.
roode, n., the cross, 258, 269.
roume, n., space, leisure, 444.
roumede, v., cleared (the place for them), 3p.sg.pt., 597
 (*OED room*, v1, sense 2).
roungede, v., roared, cried out, 3p.sg.pt., 361.
route, n., company, 531.

sacren, v., ordain, consecrate, 302; 3p.sg.pt., 'sacrede',
 300.
sad, adj., massive. firmly fixed, 258.
same, adv., together, 120.
Sarras, the city of Eualac, 55, 417, 616, 668.
sarrest, adj. as n., sorest, worst, 620.
Sarsyns, Saracens, 55.
saues, v., saves, redeems, 3p.sg.pr., 197.
sauh, see *seo*.
sauor, n., fragrance, 658.
sawes, n., predictions, 618.
sayȝ, see *seo*.
scaþe, n., harm, injury, 222.
scaþet, pp., harmed, 61.
schaft, n., shaft, 510.
schal, v., shall, 3p.sg.pr., 47, 352, 355, etc.; 'schul',
 45; (who) shall, 82; 2p.sg.pr., 'schaltou' (for shalt
 thou), 104; 'schalt', 82, 351, 612; shall (come), 611;
 2p.sg.pt., 'scholdest', 641; must, should, 3p.sg.pt.,
 'scholde', 302, 447, 463; can, could, 1p.sg.pt.,
 'scholde', 83; 3p.sg.pt., 107, 448; would, might,
 3p.sg.pt., 'scholde', 224, 321, 323, 637.
schalkene, n.gen.pl., of men, of warriors, 510.
schapes, v., designs, shapes, 3p.sg.pr., 445.
scharpe, n., swords, weapons, 513.
scheld, n., shield, 445, 559, 680; 'scheldes', plural, 508,
 516.
schendschupe, n., ignominy, dishonour, 496.
schene, adv., brightly, 510.
scheuȝ, v., give, sg.imper., 587 (*OED show*, v., sense 5).

schindringe, n., cutting, shattering, 513.
schon, n., shoes, 423.
schon , v., shone, 3p.sg.pt., 510.
schone, v., refuse battle, 496.
scute, adj., scant, tiny, 71.
seche, v., seek, 15; go, advance, rise, 528; 2p.sg.pr., 655; 2p.sg.pt., 'souȝtes', 431; 3p.sg.pt., 'souȝte', 634; 1p.pl.pt., 636, 3p.pl.pt., 'souȝten', 594; pp., 'souht', 181; came to (punishment), 3p.sg.pt., 'souȝte', 241; 2p.pl.pt., 'souȝtest', 4.
seemede, v., was fair, right, 3p.sg.pl., 115; seemed, 'semede', 183; suited (or perhaps seemed), 'semed', 564; was seen, 3p.sg.pr., 'seemes', 292.
seete, n., seat, 292.
sege, n., throne, 292.
seih, *seiȝ*, *seiȝen*, see *seo*.
seiȝe, v., to say, 142, 598, 631; 'sei', 73, 157; 'seie', 161; 'seye', 129, 199, 348; 'seyn', 70; 'sigge', 200; 1p.sg.pr., 'seiȝe', 309; 'sei', 127, 341; 'seie', 340; 2p.sg.pr., 'seist', 120; 'siggest', 352; 3p.sg.pr., 'seis', 1, 65, 74, etc.; 'seiþ', 419, 672; 'sigges', 209, 228; 3p.pl.pr., 'seiȝen', 3; 'sein', 318; 1p.sg.pt., 'seide', 124; 2p.sg.pt., 'seidest', 224, 435, 618; 3p.sg.pt., 'seide', 21, 83, 169, etc.
selli, adv., very, excessively, 94.
selue, adj., same, 303.
semblaunt, n., appearance, 65: 'or semblaunt is feble', i.e. you look to be in a bad way.
semeli, adj., pleasant, attractive, 192.
semely, adv., becomingly, decently, 636.
sence, n., incense, 290.
sencers, n., censers, 289.
sende, v., send, 115, 637, 654; sends, 3p.sg.pr.subj., 666; sent, 3p.sg.pt., 77, 483, 528; has sent, 3p.sg.pt., 460, 590.
seo, v., to see, 167, 192, 352, etc.; 'iseo', 498; 1p.sg.pr., 'seo', 138; 3p.sg.pr., 'seos', 258; 3p.sg.pt., 'sauh', 269, 276; 'say', 274; 'sayȝ', 152; 'seih', 181; 'seiȝ', 58, 112, 204, etc.; 'seȝe', 200; 3p.pl.pt., 'seȝen', 282, 283, 688; 'seiȝen', 15, 90; (fore) sei[ȝ]en' = saw before (them), 208 (see note); pp., 'seyȝen', 323; 'iseȝe', 349.
Seraphe, Eualac's brother-in-law, 456, 479, 492, etc.; Seraphe's, 539.
seruede, v., deserved, 3p.sg.pt., 482; pp., 'serued', treated, 526.
serwe, n., sorrow, 705.

seten, v., sat, 2p.pl.pt., 432; 3p.sg.pt., 'sette him',
    (refl.), 671.
seue, num., seven, 95, 574; 'seuene', 541.
seueþe, adj., seventh, 577.
seyne, n., sign, device, 197.
sigge, siggest, see *seiʒe*.
signede, v., signified, marked, 3p.sg.pt., 185.
signefies, v., means, 3p.sg.pr., 349; 'signefyes', 627;
    3p.pl.pr., 'signefyen', 301.
siker, adj., secure, 475, 605.
siker, adv., truly, indeed, 705; 'syker', 664; 'sikerli',
    541; 'sikerliche', 574; 'sikerly', 654.
sikermesse, n., security, guarantee, 623.
sitte, v., to fit, be consistent, 120; to be efficacious,
    224.
siþen, (1) conj., since, 4;
    (2) adv., then, next, 9, 12, 207, etc.
skil, n., argument, power of reasoning, 71.
slauht, n., killing, 266; 'slauʒt', i.e. crucifixion, 284.
sle, v., to slay, 94, 364; 3p.pl.pr. (or pp.), 'slen',
    517; 2p.sg.pt., 'slouʒ', 433; 3p.pl.pt., 'slowen',
    605; pp., 'islawe', 96; 'slayen', 541.
sonde, n., message, 470; dispensation, 323.
sone, adv., soon, 26, 88, 229, 324, 351, 498, 544;
    immediately, 41, 287, 294, 365, 455, 462, 516, 629,
    674; 'soone', 289.
sone, n., son, 22, 43, etc.
Sonenday, n., Sunday, 1.
sore, n., trouble, 449.
sore, adj., sore, injured, 690.
sore, adv., bitterly, 487; grievously, 542, 610.
soþe, n., truth, 523.
souht, souʒt, see *seche*.
sound, n., safety, 675.
souwe, v., sew, 427.
space, n., opportunity, 344, 580.
spedes, v., helps, 3p.sg.pr., 148; baptised, pp., 'sped', 9.
spodli, adv., successfully, 580.
spice, n., species, 193.
sporn, n., tumble, fall, 581.
spreynden, v., sprinkled, 3p.pl.pt., 314 (*OED sprenge*, v.).
sprong, v., sprang, i.e. pressed hard, 3p.sg.pt., 343;
    came from, originated (metaphoric), 3p.sg.pt., 123;
    'sprongen', 3p.pl.pt., 55; pp., 193, (cf. 123).
spute, v., dispute, 148.
sputison, n., disputation, argument, 343 (only example in
    OED).

stad, pp., 'ben stad', stand, are positioned, 397 (*OED stead*, v., sense 4).
starte, v., leapt, sprang, 3p.sg.pt., 544; jumped, 'sturten', 3p.pl.pt., 363.
starf, v., died, 3p.pl.pt., 514.
stiken, pp., pierced, 273.
stille, adv., constantly, 492, 701.
stoffes, v., marshals, 3p.sg.pr., 601 (*OED stuff*, v., sense 1c).
stor, n., supplies, provisions, possessions, 456.
stounde, n., time, 644.
stour, n., battle, 518; press, tumult, 548; 'stoures' (plur.), fights, 507.
strei3ten, v., hurried off, 3p.pl.pt., 'awei strei3ten', 456; outstretched, pp., 'streiht', 519; 'strau3t', 560; reached for, 3p.sg.pt., 'strei3te to', 544.
str[iu]en, v., to fight, 507 (see note).
strok, v., struck, 3p.sg.pt., 567; pp., 'striken', 519, 578, 679.
stude, n., place, 578; 'studes', pl., 634.
studefast, adj. for adv., constantly, resolutely, 220.
sturede, v., stirred, moved, 3p.sg.pt., 567.
summe, n., some (of them), 30; some (thing), 349 (n. or adv.).
summe, n., total, 95.
Surye, Syria, 431.
suwen (on), v., follow, 3p.pl.pr., 668.
swelten, v., die, 377.
swengeden, v., rushed, 3p.pl.pt., 529; 3p.sg.pt., 'swyngede', 576.
sweuene, n., dream, 441.
swiþe, adv., quickly, 27, 451, 571; soon, 161; much, 235.
swoune, n., swoon, 583.

take, v., capture, i.e. find fault with, 329; took, 3p.sg. pt., 'tok', 149, 632.
teeme, n., theme, text, 149.
teis, n., fastenings, cords, 504.
tei3, v., went, 3p.sg.pt., 57; went (for), i.e. chose, 3p.sg.pt., 'tei', 149 (*OED tee*, v1, sense 16); pulled, dragged, 'towen', 3p.pl.pt., 374.
Tholomer, King of Babylon, 353, 392, 404, etc.
tides, tydes, see *tyden*.
titli, adv., quickly, 575.
tobarst, v., broke into pieces, 3p.sg.pt., 384; 3p.pl.pt., 'toborsten', 509.
toclouen, pp., split, broken, 516.

tohurles, v., strikes (down), 3p.sg.pr., 533.
tornen, v., convert, 23; 'torne', 667; 'turne', 59, 312; 1p.sg.pr., 'turne', 215; pp., 'itornd', 216; become converted, 'torne', 229; 3p.sg.pt., 'tornede', 179; 3p.pl.pt., 'torneden', 304; turn (motion), 3p.pl.pt., 'tornede', 454; come, 'turne', infin., 51; changed, 3p.sg.pt., 'tornde', 684.
towen, see *teiʒ*.
trayed, pp., betrayed, 102 (*OED tray*, v.).
trayse, v., betray, deceive, 624 (*OED traise*, v.).
treo, n., tree, 39; plural, 'treos', [181], 191.
trouwe, v., believe, 1p.sg.pr., 169, 216; sg.imper., 184; 2p.sg.pr., 'trouwest', 372; 'trouwestou' (for trowest þou), 617.
tulten, v., fell over, were overthrown, 3p.pl.pt., 100 (*OED tilt*, v1, sense 2).
twayles, n., towels, 285.
twei, num., two, 708.
tweyne, num., twain, two, 287, 670.
twies, adv., twice, 136, 520.
tyden, v., to happen, fall out, 392 (of = between); 3p.sg. pr., 'tides', in 'tides him hele?', i.e. will he be well?, 372; 'tydes ...', is he successful?, 617.
tymely, adv., early, in good time, 415.

þat, conj., so that, 545, 550; until, 457.
þauʒ, conj., though, 46; 'þeiʒ', 125, 145.
þen, conj., than, 184, 246, 592, 596, 699.
þenkes (ou), v., bethink, i.e. think, remember; pl.imper. (refl.), 493.
þenne, adv., thence, from there, 25, 368, 418, 463, 689.
þenne, adv., then, 369, 450, 537, 539, etc.; 'þenn', 700.
þer(e), (1) conj., where, 13, 17, 20, 58, 302, 350, 599; (2) adv., there, 172, 701, 709, etc.; 'þerinne', 56, 100; 'þerof', 116, 677; 'þeron', 643; 'þerto', 252.
þerate, adv., because of that, in connection with that (emphatic), 72.
þester, adj., dark, 160, 235 (? - perhaps v., archaic).
þis(e), these, 21, 29, 191, 324, 331, 337, 419, 489, 686; 'þeose', 670.
þo, those, they, 60, 511, 512.
þo, adv., then, 237, 334.
þonderde, v., (it) thundered, sg.pt., 235.
þonke, v., thank, 1p.sg.pr., 'þonke', 5; 3p.pl.pr., 'þonken', 471.
þorw, prep., through, 56, 112, etc.; 'þorwʒ', 97, 104, etc.
þou, pron., thou, you (sg.), 40, 43, 71, etc.; 'þow', 158, 163; accusative, 'þe', 41, 45, etc.; genitive, 'þi', 43, 49, 51, etc.

þou3te, v. (impersonal), it seemed, sg.pt., 114, 360, 677, 687; 'þhou3te', 606; it seems, sg.pr., 'þinkeþ', 6.
þou3tes, n., anxieties, concerns, 177.
þreo, num., three, 6, 140, 150, etc.
þreten, v., threaten, 3p.pl.pr., 46.
þridde, adj., third, 123, 180, 263.
þroly, adv., eagerly, 91.
þrowe, n., period of time, 6.
þurleden, v., transfixed, ran through, 3p.pl.pt., 509 (*OED thirl*, v.).

vche, adj., each, 194, 256, 302, 613; as n., 92; 'vchon', each one, 339.
vmbe, adv., about, around, 658; 'vmbe mong', all among, 394.
vncastes, v., undoes, takes off, 3p.sg.pr., 477.
vncouþes, n., marvels, weird events, 187.
vndo, v., explain, remedy, 1p.sg.pr., 141.
vnhoused, v., turned out (of house), 3p.pl.pt., 455.
vnhuled, pp., uncovered, 515 (*OED unhele*, v.).
vnkeueres, v., uncovers, 3p.sg.pr., 559.
vnkuynde, adj., unnatural, unloving, 242.
vnneþe, adv., at most, 540.
vnsauht, pp., distressed, 64; at enmity, 'vnsau3t', 433.
vnsely, adj., wicked, 704.
vr(e), possessive, our, 32, 164, 185, 245; 'vr', 143, 323.
vsede (of), v., took the sacrament (from), 3p.sg.pt., 660 (*OED use*, v., sense 11b).
vuel, see *euel*.

Vaspasians, Vespasian, 9. (Vespasian's father, 12, is supposedly Titus).
verrei, adj., true, 341; 'verrey', 326; adv., truly, 'verreyliche', 351; 'verreili', 448.
vestimens, n., vestments, 294, 301, 311.
vigore, n., figure, device (on the shield), 448.
viole, n., vial, vessel, 290.
vois, n., voice, 21, 38, 209, etc.

war, adj., aware, on his guard, 530.
warpes, v., opens, 3p.sg.pr., 257; cast, thrown, pp., 'iworpe', 221.
wasscheles, n., vessels, 288.
wawes, v., stirs, 3p.sg.pr., 52.
weede, n., clothing, vestment, 299.
wei, n., way, 32, 313.
wel, adj., fortunate, 33; happy, pleased, 659.
wel, adv., approximately, 165, 521.

welde, v., was dominant, 3p.sg.pt., 600 (*OED wield*, v.).
wem, n., impurity, stain, 86, 180, 211, 333.
wemmet, pp., hurt, 542; 'wemmed', 678.
wenden, v., go, 3p.pl.pr., 29, 313; 2p.sg.pr., 'wendes', 420; 3p.sg.pr., 'weendes', 53, 237; 'wendes', 546; 3p.sg.pt., 'wente', 211; 3p.pl.pt., 'wenten', 191.
weore, see *ben*.
weried, pp., wearied, 436.
werre, n., war, 436.
werret, pp., warred, 60.
whappede, v., wrapped, 3p.pl.pt., 658 (*OED wap*, v2).
whon, conj., when, 25, 31, 77, etc.
whucche, n., chest, ark, 39, 237; 'wʒucche', 267, 281 (*OED hutch*, n.).
whuche, rel.pron., which, 270, 608.
wiht, n., man, person, 196, 197.
wihtli, adv., without delay, 461 (*OED wightly*, adv.).
wisse, v., show, 32.
wite, v., to know, 443; 2p.sg.pt. as pr., 'wost', 330; 'wostou' (for 'wost þou'), 420; 3p.sg.pr.subj., 'wite', 465; 3p.sg.pt., 'wuste', 58, 677; sg.imper., 'wite', 86. See *nuste*.
witered, pp., informed, 466 (*OED witter*, v: mainly alliterative).
witerli, adv., truly, undoubtedly, 154.
wiþdrawe, v., retreat, refl., 463; take off, 'wiþdrawe þe of'; sg.imper., 311.
wiþouten, (1) adv., on the outside, externally, 316; outside, 165;
(2) prep., without, 180; 'withouten', 86, 211, 333.
wiþsaken, pp., opposed, 178.
wol, v., will, 1p.sg.pr., 621; 'wole', 'wol', 624; 2p.sg.pr., 'woltou', 646; 1p.sg.pt., 'wolde', 640; 2p.sg.pt., 'woldestou' (for 'woldest þou'), 640; 2p.pl.pt., 'wolde ʒe', 67; desired, 3p.sg.pt., 'wolde', 63, 115, 179, 359; 3p.pl.pt., 'wolden', 363.
wonde, v., hesitate, flinch, 399.
wonderli, adv., amazingly, absurdly, 106.
wondet, pp., wounded, 542; 'woundet', 555, 610.
wonen, v., to dwell, 180; 3p.sg.pt., 'wonede', 56, 635; pp., 'woned', 315 (*OED win*, v2).
wonges, n., cheeks, 647.
wood, adj., mad, 367.
worche, v., work, 49.
worþe, v., may (he) be; 3p.sg.pr.subj., 146.
woxen, v., grew, became, 2p.pl.pt., 433; 3p.pl.pt., 452.
wraþþed, pp., angry, vexed, 58.

writ, n., writing, 660.
wrouȝt, v., worked, 3p.sg.pt., 593; pp., 554; made, 3p.sg.
       pt., 'wrouȝte', 303; pp., 'wrouȝt', 204, 676;
       carried out his advice, 3p.pl.pt., 'his red
       wrouȝten', 491.
wuste, see *wite*.
wustest, v., protected, 2p.sg.pt., 221 (*OED wite*, v2).
wynt, n., wind, 658.
wȝucche, see *whucche*.

ȝaf, v., gave, 3p.sg.pt., 439.
ȝe, yes, 170, 621.
ȝeme, v., have in charge, look after, take care of, 309;
      2p.sg.pr., 'ȝemes', 310.
ȝernloker, adv., more eagerly, 593.
ȝif, conj., if, 307, 329, 339, 484; 'bote ȝif', unless, 305.
ȝitte, adv., yet, 63; 'ȝut', 357; still, 'ȝitte', 334;
      'ȝit', 305.
ȝong, adj., young, 437, 479, 593.
ȝonge, v., go, 34; 3p.pl.pr., 'ȝongen', 313, 394.
ȝor, your, 673.
ȝore, n., 'of ȝore', formerly, in olden days, 317.

DATE DUE

4-4-90			
IL:528046l			

WITHDRAWN from the Alma College Library

DEMCO 38-297